Invisible, Outlawed, and Untaxed

INVISIBLE, OUTLAWED, and UNTAXED

America's Underground Economy

HARRY I. GREENFIELD

PRAEGER

Westport, Connecticut
London

Library of Congress Cataloging-in-Publication Data

Greenfield, Harry I.
Invisible, outlawed, and untaxed : America's underground economy / Harry I. Greenfield.
p. cm.
Includes bibliographical references and index.
ISBN 0-275-94507-3 (alk. paper)
1. Informal sector (Economics)—United States. I. Title.
HD2346.U5G74 1993
330.973—dc20 92-35341

British Library Cataloguing in Publication Data is available.

Library of Congress Catalog Card Number: 92-35341
ISBN: 0-275-94507-3

First published in 1993

Praeger Publishers, 88 Post Road West, Westport, CT 06881
An imprint of Greenwood Publishing Group, Inc.

Printed in the United States of America

The paper used in this book complies with the Permanent Paper Standard issued by the National Information Standards Organization (Z39.48-1984).

10 9 8 7 6 5 4 3 2 1

To the Memory of my Parents
Sucher and Chaje Taube Greenfield and
To the Memory of my Parents-in-law
Bernard and Bessie Frohlinger

Contents

Preface xi

Acknowledgments xiii

1 Aboveground and Underground 1

Getting a Handle on the Underground Economy 1

A Suggestion for Simplifying the Concept of the Underground Economy 2

An Overview of the Underground 6

Functions and Motives 13

Who and Why 14

The Aboveground and Underground Interface 15

2 On the Trail: Monetary Clues or Cherchez le Cash 19

More Cash in a Cashless Society 19

Money Supply: The Primary Suspect 23

Blind Alley—Try Again 27

On the Wrong Trail? 29

3 **Tax Evasion and Other Behavioral Clues** 35

The Trails Diverge: Macro versus Micro 35

The Tax Beaters 36

A Partial Lifting of the Veil—Courtesy of the IRS 40

The Macro Level Once Again 44

The Micro Level: Buying and Selling in the Underground Economy 46

4 **Sectoral Clues: The Building Block Approach** 51

The Building's Framework 51

Block Number One—Drugs 52

Block Number Two—Illegal Gambling 56

Block Number Three—Prostitution and Pornography 58

Block Number Four—Illegal Abortion 61

Block Number Five—Child Pornography 62

Block Number Six—Audio, Video, and Software Piracy 62

More Blocks—Cigarette Smuggling, Loan Sharking, Bartering, and Skimming 63

The House that Estimates Built 64

Addendum 65

5 **Labor Market Clues** 73

Will the Real Underground Labor Force Stand Up and Be Counted? 73
Some Notes on the Demand and Supply of Underground Labor 75
Where Have All the Workers Gone? 76
Are They Employed? 77
What Do the Numbers Show? 78
The Employment-to-Population Ratio 83
Are They Unemployed? 84
Aliens and Moonlighters 87
Pick a Number 88

6 **A Brief Glance at the Underground Economies Abroad** 93

Forenote 93
Part I—Industrialized Nations 95
Part II—Developing and Newly Industrialized Countries 98

7 **Economic Consequences of the Underground Economy** 105

Information, Misinformation, and Disinformation 105
Procyclical, Countercyclical, or Cycle-Neutral? 109
Back to the Drawing Board 110
Resource Shifts and Economic Efficiency 113
Tax Cuts and Their Effects 114
Revenue Loss and Its Consequence 116
Tax Morality 117

Illuminating the Shadows 117

8 Trail's End: Conclusion 123

Bibliography 127

Index 135

Preface

Oats peas beans and barley grow
Oats peas beans and barley grow
Do you or I or anyone know
How oats, peas beans and barley grow?

Anon

—Do you or I or anyone know what the underground economy is?

—Do you or I or anyone know how big the underground economy is?

—Do you or I or anyone know how fast the underground economy is growing?

—Do you or I or anyone know how many people work in the underground economy?

—Do you or I or anyone know what to do about the underground economy?

I hope, in what follows, to attempt to answer or at least to indicate how to approach answers to the questions posed. The existing literature on these matters is as extensive as it is diffuse. The material ranges over domestic as well as international economies; it encompasses such diverse areas as statistical measurement, urban anthropology, criminology, psychology of deviant behavior, sociological phenomena, banking, taxation, industrial organization, and economic development. Each of these disciplines views the underground economy through its particular lens, and many valuable insights may be gleaned from them. The organizing principle in the present work, however, and its major emphasis, is on the economic aspects of underground economic activity. By providing a more precise definition of the underground economy, one that is consistent with standard and accepted economic measures, the fuzziness surrounding the concept will, it is hoped, be brought into clearer focus. We may then obtain a proper perspective from which to evaluate the many (outlandish) estimates of the size of the underground economy that appear from time to time but add little to our understanding of this phenomenon.

To the degree that our goal is achieved, the game will have been worth the candle.

Acknowledgments

I wish to express my appreciation to the personnel of the New York Public Library at 42nd Street and for the use of the Wertheim Study—both of which made the research and writing of this book a pleasurable experience.

I owe a great debt to my wife, Gladys, whose unfailing support, encouragement, and technical assistance enabled me to carry this project through to completion. The highest cost of the investment in time and effort for both of us was the quality time that could have been spent with our grandchildren.

For the all-important tasks of typing and word processing, I am deeply grateful to the following persons: Grace Romeo, Gail Frohlinger, Frieda Topf, and my daughter, Debra Stark.

I also wish to express my gratitude to James R. Dunton, Editor-in-Chief of Praeger Publishers, for his confidence in the work and to Nita Romer, Production Editor, for her valuable editorial assistance.

1

Aboveground and Underground

GETTING A HANDLE ON THE UNDERGROUND ECONOMY

The underground economy (for want of a better term) has been the subject of a number of congressional hearings, of several international conferences, and of any number of books and monographs. What have we learned from these many attempts to define it, to estimate its size, and to analyze its relationship to the general economy? A lot and a little—a lot because an area of research has been uncovered, and many heretofore obscured relationships between normal and extranormal economic activities have been brought to light—a little because there are almost as many conceptions of the underground economy as there are investigators, leaving us with a confusing array of ideas and choices with no clear direction out of the maze.

To illustrate: For one year, 1976, estimates of the size of the underground economy in the United States ranged from 1.4 percent of the GNP or $25 billion to 28 percent of the GNP or $499 billion.[1] Such a huge discrepancy is hardly likely to instill confidence either in those who did the estimating or in the very concept itself. Something is wrong here, but what is it?

Obviously, the problem lies with the definition of the term "underground economy." Unfortunately, there is, as yet, no standard definition that is used by the many researchers in the field, hence the proliferation of estimates. When we consider that, "the range of services and goods represented in the irregular economy is very broad, extending from a child's lemonade stand to the empires of organized crime,"[2] it is not surprising that finding a common thread binding all of these activities is an elusive undertaking.

A SUGGESTION FOR SIMPLIFYING THE CONCEPT OF THE UNDERGROUND ECONOMY

In a later chapter, we examine the different methods used to arrive at the various estimates, but first things first. The definition that I shall employ throughout is as follows: By the term underground economy, I mean the production and distribution of goods and services that, for the most part, are initially undetected (and therefore unrecorded) in the U.S. national income and product accounts (NIPA). The qualifying term is used initially since most of the incomes earned in the underground are ultimately spent for legitimate goods and services in the regular economy, and at that point, they are captured in the statistical net.[3]

It should be noted that some types of activity are specifically excluded from the national accounts—drugs, prostitution, and gambling—whereas other kinds are meant to be included but so far have eluded accurate measurement for example, working "off-the-books."[4]

The NIPA provides us with a single measure of all of the economic activity that takes place in a given period of time, that is, the Gross National Product or GNP. More specifically, the GNP is defined as the market value of all the goods and services produced in a given time period (with adjustments for inventories, and exports and imports)—all, that is, except illegal activities, such as the production and distribution of drugs, prostitution (except where legal), gambling (except where legal), and as mentioned above, "off-the-books" activity. The latter consists mostly of legal production that is hidden from regulatory agencies and tax authorities, a perfect example of which surfaced in a *New York Times* article on the illegal mining of Kentucky coal by so-called wildcatters. The article noted that "wildcat miners fatten their profits by skirting safety and land use regulations, taxes and other government imposed constraints."[5]

Those of us who have taught at any level know that students are more interested in exceptions than they are in rules, and this case is no exception. The usual questions are: Why are these activities excluded, and how much would GNP be increased if they were included? (It should be pointed out here that some perfectly legal and necessary types of production, such as the value of housewives' services in the home—the rearing of children, shopping, cooking, and cleaning—and even the value of do-it-yourself activities, are not, included in GNP calculations; such activities are viewed as not-for-market production.)

Two questions suggest themselves at this point regarding the illegal activities mentioned above: Should they be included in the measurement of our total economic activity, and if so, how do we go about measuring them? In note 4, we indicated Simon Kuznets' answer to the first question, namely that it is an arbitrary decision based on societal norms and values. In this connection, Bruno Stein has pointed out that "most of the world is . . . using a national accounting system that, at least in principle, covers illegal as well as legal activities,"[6] thus complicating international comparisons.

As to the second question—how to measure—after all, an individual who files an IRS 1040 form will not generally disclose the fact that he (or she) is a drug dealer or that she (or he) is a prostitute. Furthermore, what about those who do not file income tax returns, who do not bother to register their "businesses" with the appropriate authorities (certificates of incorporation, license requirements, and the like), and who do not, as a result, pay sales, excise, or payroll taxes? In short, how do we go about measuring what individuals (or corporations) wish to conceal from the tax collectors or from the statistical sleuths of the Census, Labor, or Commerce Departments? If there is no "paper trail," we can not easily follow the culprits.

Returning to our definition, recall that in the GNP, we measure only output that is currently produced. Thus, sales of secondhand cars are not included in the GNP, since the cars were counted in their year of production. However, the income earned in legitimate sales activities is taxable and is included in the GNP. The "output" in this case comes under the heading of services rather than of goods. Similarly, all forms of theft are not included in the GNP, since theft results in the redistribution of existing assets (previously measured), and not the production of new goods and services. *B* stealing from *A* simply redistributes income or property (real and intellectual) from *A* to *B* without any change taking place in national income or output, or money in circulation.

One of the most common errors made by writers in this field is to equate tax evasion with the underground economy. Carla Tighe states flatly that "any income-generating activity that is not taxed is part of the underground economy."[7] Not so. A mugger who empties wallets on a subway car is surely generating income for himself and most assuredly is not taxed, but as we pointed out, this kind of activity should not be construed as being part of the underground economy. In a similar vein, a person who sells stolen goods is generating income that is not taxed, and an unlicensed curbside vendor who sells old paperbacks is in the same category: Illegal, yes; part of the underground economy, no. Nonfiling of tax returns when they should be filed or underreporting of income by those who do file are activities that may or may not fall under the rubric of the underground economy. We should attempt, in our statistical net, to capture only income that was earned in the underground economy and not recorded (at the time of production) in the GNP.

Viewed from this perspective, the huge S&L (Savings and Loan) debacle is not part of the underground economy. In this case, a banker may have loaned a developer $100 million. Let us assume that the developer builds a shopping mall that fails as a business enterprise. What are the results? The developer may have paid himself an enormous salary (which he may or may not report to the IRS); the labor and materials used in the construction of the mall are recorded as legitimate business expenses, and the bank posts a loss of $100 million (assuming no recovery from the sale of the mall) in its financial statements. All of these actions are recorded, one way or another (except for the nonfiler) in our national accounts hence no underground economy. Another way of stating these matters is that not all criminal activity is part of the underground economy, but all activities in the underground economy are, by definition, criminal.

Omitting redistributive activities—recall A and B above—will result in much lower estimates of the size of the underground economy than many of those to which we have been exposed in learned journals and in the media. This explains a good deal of the discrepancies in the size of the underground economy that were noted at the outset. Our view, however, is consistent with that in the national income accounting system and is more meaningful from an economic standpoint. If one wishes to calculate just how much of the GNP is missing as a result of the underground economy and then to relate that sum to the GNP in the form of a ratio, then both the numerator and the denominator must be part of the same universe, so to speak. Otherwise, we will be dividing apples by oranges—an all too common phenomenon in this area.

It comes down to a matter of choice: One can take the view that all illegal or criminal economic activities (burglary, arson, embezzlement, and white-collar crimes) together with the standard types, such as drugs, gambling, and prostitution, comprise the underground economy. There can be no quarrel with those who take that point of view as long as what is included in the scope of underground activities is made explicit, in which case, problems arising from the comparability of various estimates can be largely eliminated. Admittedly, the more sensational the number so derived, the more appealing it is to the media. The view advanced here, eschews sensationalism for meaningfulness and consistency.

AN OVERVIEW OF THE UNDERGROUND

A simple series of block diagrams may help to place the underground economy in perspective. In what follows, these symbols are used:

H = Households
F = Firms
G = Government
NFP = Not-For-Profit
U.E. = Underground Economy

A.

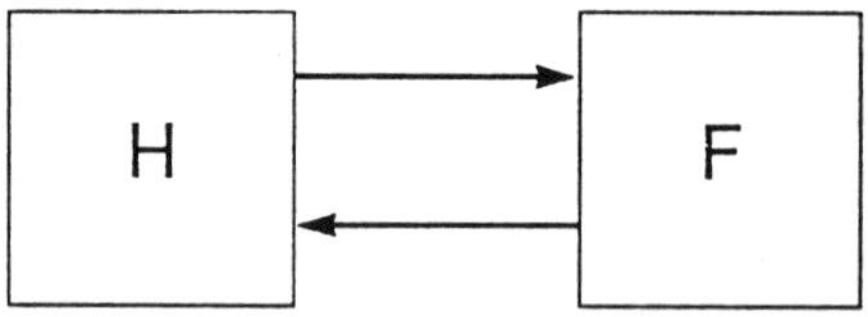

Two sectors are shown here: households and firms. Households supply services (mostly labor inputs) to the firms, which then supply goods and services to the households. The firms make wage payments to the households which then use the income to purchase goods and services from the firms.

B.

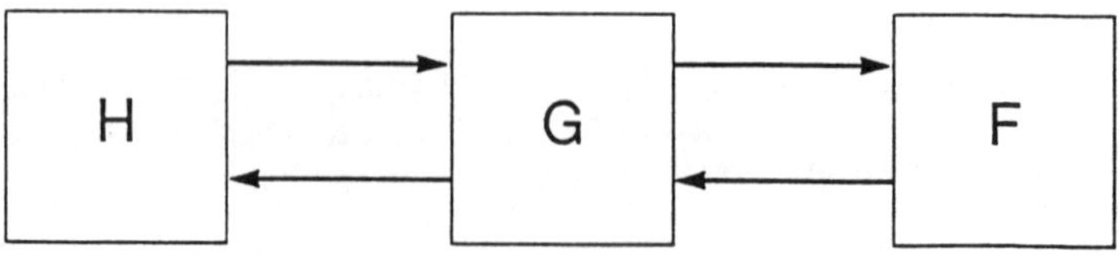

In B the government sector is added. Households pay taxes to the government in return for various goods and services. Likewise, firms pay taxes to the government for various goods and services they seek.

C.

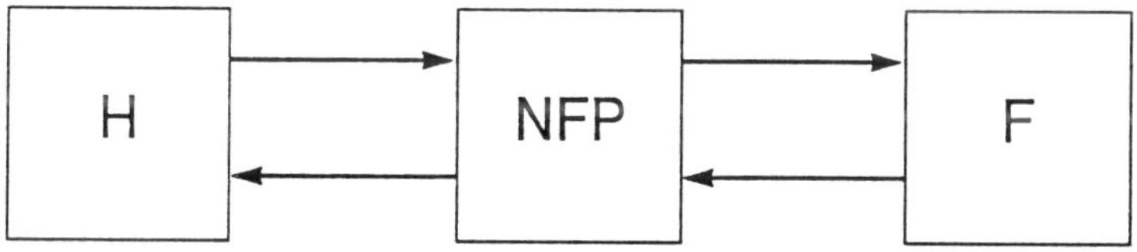

In C, a Not-For-Profit sector is added (libraries, museums, Red Cross, research foundations, boy and girl scouts). Households and firms supply funds (philanthropy) to the NFP sector, which, in turn, supplies both sectors with such services as were mentioned. The NFP sector does not, as a rule, pay taxes to the government, hence the omission of the G sector.

D.

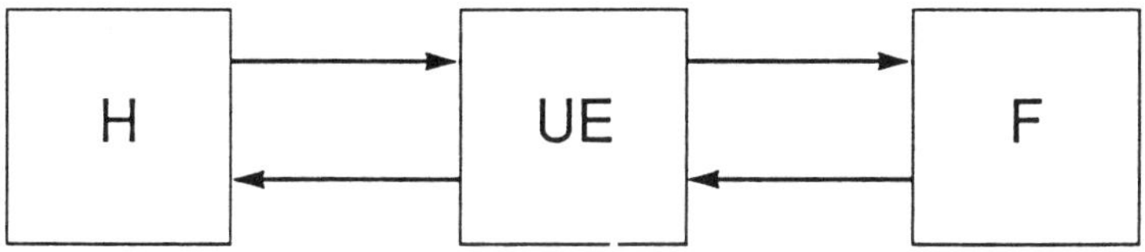

In D, the underground economy is shown as a sector. In return for certain goods and services from U.E. (drugs, prostitution, gambling), household supply that sector with funds. Similarly, the U.E. supplies firms with goods and services and labor inputs for "off-the-books" activity. The U.E. also purchases capital equipment from F (cars, offices, weapons). Since the raison d'être of the U.E. is primarily tax evasion, we do not show the interaction with G.

Now, what exactly is in the U.E. box? Recalling our earlier discussion, there are only two types of underground activity: illegal production and illegal redistribution. The former is defined by legislation, for example, the production of alcoholic beverages was prohibited by the eighteenth Amendment (hence removed from the GNP); the twenty-first Amendment some fifteen years later re-

Table 1.1
A Typology of Underground Activities

Definitely Underground	Marginally Underground	Illegal, But Not Part of Underground
(1)	(2)	(3)
Production and distribution of drugs Prostitution Off-the-Books production of goods and services Child Pornography Illegal Abortions Video Piracy	Illegal Gambling Loan Sharking Barter Do-it-Yourself Skimming Cigarette Smuggling	Theft of all kinds: Personal, household, Automobile, Employee Theft, Robbery, Burglary, Arson Counterfeiting, Computer and White Collar Crime (e.g. Securities Fraud)

pealed the eighteenth, thus reinstating alcohol in the GNP. As for the latter, one can speak of legal redistribution, for example, the attempt to achieve greater equality in income distribution via the tax system, or illegal redistribution of income or assets via theft. Since redistributive activities (legal or illegal) are not included in the GNP, this leaves illegal production of goods and services as the one category that properly ought to be considered as comprising the underground economy. In Table 1.1 the kinds of activity listed in columns 1 and 2 qualify for inclusion as underground economic activity; those in column three do not.

A further word is warranted concerning the entries in this table. The first item in column 1, the production and distribution of drugs, fits the definitions in our GNP accounts, namely, that a commodity has been produced (and a corresponding service of distribution) in a given time period. If drugs were legalized, their value would be part of the GNP, but since in the United States they are not, we place them in the underground economy.

Much the same reasoning applies to prostitution and child pornography. Here we are dealing with services instead of goods, but GNP, as we know, includes both. If prostitution were legalized (as it is in some countries and in some counties in the United States), the value of such services would be included in GNP, but since it is not legal and therefore not recorded, we place it underground. It is difficult to conceive of child pornography being legalized—it will always remain as a most pernicious underground activity.

"Off-the-books" activity is, by definition, excluded from the GNP. Goods and/or services are produced, but neither the entrepreneur (be he or she a self-employed individual or a corporation) nor the employee records the production or the income earned in the process. There are a multitude of examples: home repairs paid for in cash; tutoring; baby sitting; appliance and automobile repairs; unlicensed curbside vendors and farmers who sell part of their output for cash. To the extent that the "off-the-bookers" buy materials (wood, paint, tools) in the legitimate marketplace, such purchases will, of course, be recorded and included in GNP. What is missing, however, is the so-called value-added to those materials by the labor of the employee or the self-employed entrepreneur. What we have here is legal output by illegal means, hence its position in the underground.

The categories of illegal gambling and loan sharking are placed in the marginal column for the reason that they partake both of a redistributive and a productive kind of activity. Gambling, basically, is a zero-sum game, that is, one side gains what the other side loses with no additional output forthcoming in the process. On this ground, it would not be counted in the GNP, but there is another aspect to it—the service of recreation. Where gambling is legal, as in the casinos of Las Vegas and Atlantic City, or in the Off Track Betting parlors, the recreational aspect is most noticeable, although financial gain is undoubtedly the dominant motive. Of course, legalized gambling—that is the profits minus the skimming—would be included in the national income accounts, but other forms of gambling, like numbers, athletic contests, and cock-fighting, are "unseen." With some hesitation, but with the weight of convention on our side, we include illegal gambling as part of the underground economy.

The case of loan sharking is similar. Lending money is the major activity of legitimate enterprises, such as banks and finance companies, and as such, it is very much a part of GNP. Loan sharking, however, consists of lending money at exorbitant rates of interest. (What is exorbitant depends on time, place, and usury laws). Because it so closely resembles the legitimate function of other lending institutions and because the profits are not recorded, we consider loan sharking to be part of the underground economy.

Barter arrangements also present a dichotomy. Bartering of existing assets—my snow blower for your power saw—would not be included in the GNP accounts. Bartering of newly created goods or services, however—dental services for legal services, for example—would be included in the national accounts if they were purchased as normal market transactions. Moreover, the income earned by the dentist and lawyer would have to be declared to the IRS, but since no payments were made—either by check or by cash—there would be no record of the transaction. To the extent that we may be able to differentiate barter arrangements as between those that involve newly created goods and services and those that do not, we would be able to include the former in estimates of the underground economy. Since services, by definition, cannot be inventoried, they are newly created and, hence, part of the underground economy.

Do-it-yourself activities are often included in studies of the underground economy for the reason that new goods and/or services are currently produced, but this activity, being "invisible," is not recorded in our GNP. Examples of such activities are a homeowner who builds an extension on his house (without permit), builds bookcases, repairs his own car or TV set, or mows his own lawn.

These cases are similar to the "off-the-books" discussion above, with the exception that no "books" are involved, though the individual can technically be considered as self-employed. Our discussion of the work of housewives is also germane here. If the homeowner in our illustration buys materials in the normal market, such purchases of course become part of the GNP. What is not recorded, again, is the value added to the materials by the do-it-yourselfer. No taxes are paid on the value of the new goods and services produced, except for the excise and/or sales taxes paid on the materials purchased on the open market. The term "underground" has a pejorative connotation, and one is reluctant to apply that term to do-it-yourself activities, but since the criterion of current output not recorded is met in this case, we shall include it, to the extent that estimates are available, in our underground economy total.

Skimming, the act of not recording a portion of sales or revenues, may or may not be part of the underground economy, hence its place in the marginal column. The distinction turns on who does the skimming. When an employee manages not to record all of the sales or revenues received and pockets the unrecorded amount, he or she is, in effect, reducing the potential profit of the employer. From this perspective, employee skimming or "fiddling," as the British call it, is a form of involuntary income redistribution—from the employer to the employee. On the other hand, when an employer fails to record all of the revenues from an enterprise in order to evade taxes, this may be viewed as a form of "off-the-books" activity, that is, revenues derived from the production or distribution of legitimate goods or services that is not recorded in the national income accounts—hence part of the underground economy. Should the employer and the employee be in cahoots, the revenue, if it can be estimated, should be halved—one half in the underground and one half not.

One tax evasion stratagem is dual record keeping; the real output of the firm, as opposed to the output stated for tax purposes, is recorded in the second set of books. The difference between the numbers in the two sets of books represents the firm's underground activity.

In the case of cigarette smuggling, we have an activity involving legally produced goods (which are included in the GNP) combined with their illegal sale and distribution in order to evade state excise and federal income taxes. The fact that the distributive activities are unseen and untaxed places that part of the operation in the underground economy. The smugglers, in effect, are working "off-the-books." The same principle applies to liquor, gasoline, and other goods subject to excise and/or sales taxes.

Now to the third column—items that are excluded (by our definitions) from the underground economy. As was explained earlier, purely redistributive activities—zero-sum games—are not included in GNP, since no new production of goods or services is generated. In fact, in the case of arson, goods are actually destroyed. When an employee steals goods, services, time from an employer, the result is a diminution of profit of the latter and an unrecorded increase in income (the value of what was stolen) to the former. The same principle applies to all of the other forms of theft—they are all illegal and unrecorded, but they are not, on those accounts, part of the underground economy.

To summarize: The aboveground or normal economy consists of the legal production of goods and services that are measured (plus or minus statistical sampling errors) in our national income and product accounts. As was pointed out above, some illegal types of output are also captured by the GNP. For instance, when a drug dealer uses some of his income to purchase a new car, such purchases are recorded as consumer expenditures in the national accounts—provided the transaction was not a cash, under-the-table type of deal. (There is, however, no corresponding entry on the income side of the accounts.) Secondly, there is a category of economic activity that consists of legal output but is not caught in our statistical net, namely "off-the-books" activity. Finally, there is economic activity that is both illegal and unmeasured (for example, drugs).

Succinctly put, we have:

1. legal and measured economic activity,
2. legal and unmeasured economic activity and
3. illegal and unmeasured economic activity.

The underground economy, in our view is comprised of items two and three.

A British economist, Derek Blades, has produced a simple diagram, that goes to the core of the matter:

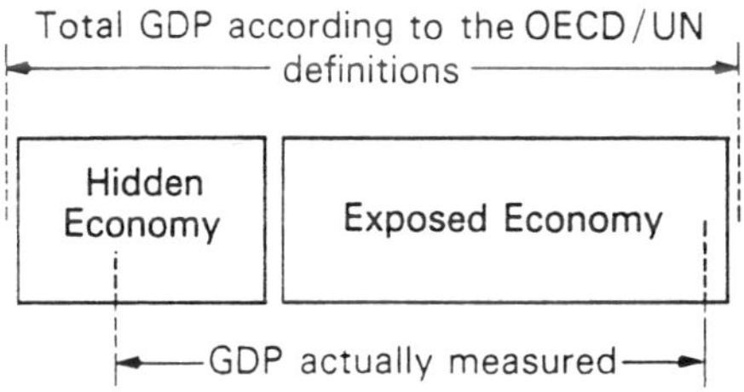

Source: Derek Blades, "The Hidden Economy and National Accounts," *OECD Observer*, January 1982, p. 15. Reprinted with permission.

Blades points out that:

1. some of the hidden economy is included in the national accounts;
2. some of the legal output that should be measured is not because of some holes in the statistical net; and
3. the "hidden economy"' concept should be consistent with what GNP intends to measure and not items that are intentionally omitted. (*See*, however, Chapter 4, where such items are included.)

FUNCTIONS AND MOTIVES

There is no precise demarcation among the three groups mentioned above. Instead, there are various points where the aboveground and the underground economies interact. It has been pointed out, for instance, that in the Soviet Union and in other command-type economic systems, the normal economy could hardly exist without the output and flexibility provided by their so-called "second economies." As Hedrick Smith, a long-time student of the Soviet system, stated, "parallel to the official economy there exists an entire thriving counter-economy [which] has become an integral part of the Soviet system, a built-in, permanent feature of Soviet society."[8] With the disintegration of the central nucleus and the formation of the Confederation of Independent States, the underground economy will doubtless become even more pervasive. The same holds true of the so-called "informal economies" of underdeveloped and developing economies. In the latter case, the informal economy provides employment opportunities that are not available, for one reason or another, in the legal economy.[9]

Some have viewed underground activity in general as a sort of safety value, in the absence of which there would be much more political and social instability. Further, some writers, wrongly I believe, view underground economic activity as a form of class warfare, a means of affecting revolutionary change in the socio-political system.

Philip Mattera, for example, states that "a profound power shift in class relations is taking place and the informal economy is contributing mightily to it."[10] A sociologist has opined, "It could be argued that what is denounced as a 'parasitic' underground economy in the U.S. is actually the way that working people defend themselves against the attacks on their standard of living characteristic of mature capitalism."[11] Also, two anthropologists see a conspiracy: "In the discourse of politicians and civil servants, notions of a separate economy are used to disguise real social problems, to tinker with unemployment statistics and to legitimate punitive welfare policies."[12]

Idealogues are often carried away by what they think they see. In truth, many of those who are engaged in underground economic activity are simply taking advantage of the interstices that exist in the "normal" economy, and they might resist, very strongly, any systemic change that would deprive them of their means of livelihood. This factor is especially important in less developed countries.

WHO AND WHY

Some "players" in the underground economy are in it for the thrill of doing something illegal by flaunting the authorities. Without delving into the psychological pathology of those so motivated,[13] my view is that the number of such undergrounders is minimal. The primary motive is money—trite as this may seem as an explanatory variable. The dominant motives for participating in the underground economy are: the potential for huge monetary gains, as in the drug trade; high marginal tax rates; the perception of unfairness in the tax system (millionaires and large corporations with no or low tax liabilities; the feeling (and perhaps the knowledge) that tax cheating is ubiquitous; the need to earn income by those who are unemployed or to supplement inadequate wages, pensions, or other income; and the desire to evade what are considered to be unfair and stifling governmental rules and regulations.

THE ABOVEGROUND AND UNDERGROUND INTERFACE

As mentioned earlier, there is a dynamic interaction between the normal and extranormal economies. Some people may participate in the underground economy at one time but not another, and some who are employed in the aboveground economy may participate on a part-time basis at one time (moonlighting) or on a full-time basis at other times. Then again, there may be some more or less permanent players with well-defined organizational structures, such as the Maffia-type crime syndicates. In this connection, I do not hold with the view of Philip Mattera that "the underground cannot be strictly separated from the underworld."[14] Not only can the two be separated, but they must be in the interest of consistency and economic understanding. The underworld players are primarily, if not wholly, engaged in illegal redistributive-type activities (theft, embezzlement, extortion). Only those underworld activities that result in the new production of goods or services should be included in the underground economy—for example, the growing and sale of illicit drugs. In all cases, as Frank Cowell so pithily stated, "Hijackers, whores and hit men, all weigh the prospective costs and benefits of their labors."[15]

Shifting of resources from the aboveground to the underground economies and vice versa may be a function of a number of factors, such as changes in law enforcement activities; changes in marginal tax rates; legislative changes (for example, Prohibition repealed); changes in tastes (more or less drug use); fear of disease, as in the relationship between prostitution and AIDS; inflation rates; changes in relative prices—(if and when plumbers charges are $200 per hour, many homeowners will become amateur plumbers; conversely, if plumbers were to charge $2.00 per hour [assuming no productivity change], few homeowners would own even a plunger); and finally, general economic conditions.

In the foregoing, a suggestion for simplifying the concept of the underground economy was presented. In what follows, I shall attempt to flesh out this framework with some data and to analyze the economic ramifications of this (partly) invisible subeconomy.

NOTES

1. W. C. Boeschoten and M.M.G. Fase, "The Volume of Payments and Informal Economy of the Netherlands," *Monetary Monographs*, No. 1, De Nederlandsche Bank, Martinus Nijhoff Publishers, Dordrecht, p. 34 and Economic Report of the President (Feb. 1990): 294. *See* also, Carol S. Carson, "The Underground Economy: An Introduction," *Survey of Current Business* 64 (May 1984) especially Table 3, p. 33. Dr. Carson's two articles (the second was in July 1984) constitute, in my view, the best survey of the field.

2. Louis A. Ferman and Louise E. Berndt, "The Irregular Economy," in *Can I Have It in Cash*, ed. Stuart Henry (London: Astragal Books, 1981), 28.

3. For a systematic exposition of the national accounts, *see* Carol S. Carson, "Gross National Product and Related Measures," in *The Handbook of Economic and Financial Measures*, ed. Frank J. Fabozzi and Harry I. Greenfield, (Homewood, Ill.: Dow Jones, Irwin, 1984), 3 and following.

4. The rationale for excluding certain activities was explained by Simon Kuznets, arguably the "father" of our national accounting system:

In the statistical measurement of national income the question reduces itself to what commodities and services should be excluded because, by and large, they do not contribute to the goal of economic activity—satisfaction of consumers wants. Specific examples may range from services such as are rendered Mr. Smith by a professional gang of killers in disposing of his rival Mr. Jones, to commodities such as harmful drugs or useless patent medicines. Simon Kuznets, "National Income: A Summary of Findings," *National Bureau of Economic Research* (1946): 121.

5. *New York Times*, March 3, 1991, 1.

6. Bruno Stein, "Subterranean Labor Markets: A Conceptual Analysis," in *The Economics of the Shadow Economy*, Proceedings of the International Conference on the Economics of the Shadow Economy, held at the University of Bielefeld, West Germany, October 10–14, 1983, ed. W. Gaertner and A. Wenig, 1985, p. 47.

7. Carla Tighe, "The Underground Economy," *Illinois Business Review* (April 1985): 10.

8. Quoted in Philip Mattera, *Off-The Books: The Rise of the Underground Economy* (New York: St. Martin's Press, 1985), 111.

9. *The Urban Informal Sector in Developing Countries*, ed. S. V. Sethuramen (Geneva: International Labour Office, 1981).

10. Philip Mattera, *Off the Books*, n. 6, 39.

11. "Visions of Power: Ideology and Practice in the American Garage Sale." The authors go on to state that "it is arguable that underground and irregular economic forms are basic mechanisms of contemporary working-class social reproduction." Stephen S. Soiffer and Gretchen M. Hermann, *Sociological Review* 35 (Feb. 1987): 49–50.

12. Philip Harding and Richard Jenkins, *The Myth of the Hidden Economy* (University Press, 1989), 148.

13. *See* Sigmund Freud, "Civilization and Its Discontents," in *A Freud Reader*, ed. Peter Gay (ed.) (New York: W. W. Norton, 1989), 722 and following.

14. Mattera, *Off the Books*, 65.

15. Frank A. Cowell, *Cheating the Government* (Cambridge, Mass.: MIT Press, 1990), 3.

2

On the Trail: Monetary Clues or Cherchez le Cash

MORE CASH IN A CASHLESS SOCIETY

In spite of the fact that most underground economic activity leaves no paper trail (check stubs, invoices, or receipts), economists and others have attempted to ferret out the amount of such activity by indirect means. More specifically, the focus of such efforts has been to try to estimate underground activity by analyses of the quantity and composition of cash held by the public—as distinct from that held, for instance, by the Treasury, the Federal Reserve Banks, and in the vaults of depository institutions. If the trend over the past decades has been moving toward the greater use of checks, credit cards, and electronic fund transfers, we should expect to find a diminution (on a per capita basis) in the amount of cash held by the public. Instead, we find the opposite—an increase in the per capita holdings of such cash.

Not too long ago, I purchased a birthday gift for a friend—with my credit card, of course, at Bloomingdales department store in New York City. Being curious, I asked the clerk at the cash register for his estimate of the number of sales made by credit card versus those made by cash. He answered unhesitatingly—about 90 95 percent. Now, although one cannot infer from this one counter what the experience of all the other counters in the store is with respect to credit card purchases, everyday observation confirms that there has been a sea-change over the past decade or so in the way consumer purchases are made, that is, a move from real to plastic money. More than nine years ago, the Board of Governors of the Federal Reserve System found, for example, that "in 1983, 64 percent of U.S. families held at least one credit card" and that "only a small proportion of families reported never using credit cards."[1] RAM Research, a credit card research company, reports that "credit cards have been used by Americans since 1915 and are now a $366 billion annual business in the United States."[2] One writer has gone as far as to suggest that electronic fund transfers "will significantly decrease the amount of money held by the average individual. Money, as we know it, will lose its present form, paper currency will give way to electronic impulses."[3] Indeed, a major step in this direction is in the planning stage. A *Wall Street Journal* report indicates that an Automatic Teller Machine group is looking into the possibility of establishing a national debit card system that would allow consumers to deduct purchases from supermarkets instantly from their checking accounts.[4]

There are a host of other reasons for the expectation of a decrease in the rise of currency. J.R.S. Revell of the (Organization for Economic Co-operation and Development) OECD, for instance, stated that "the growth in crime has been one of the factors leading to the rise of checks and credit cards for very small transactions in certain countries because it enables people to carry less cash on their persons."[5] The same author points also to the increasing use of bank transfers for the payment of salaries as well as to the emerging use of personal computers in the home for banking transactions.

In view of all of these reasons for not holding cash, as well as some others to be discussed shortly, why then do we find the persistent and seemingly perverse growth in currency held by the public? A *Wall Street Journal* piece addressed some of the answers: the fact that illegal immigrants prefer, for obvious reasons, to keep their earnings in cash rather than in banks; the fact that among some sections of the populace, there has traditionally been a distrust of banks (strengthened in recent days, no doubt, by the huge number of bank failures brought on by the S&L scandal); the desire by one spouse not to reveal some income to the other; and finally, psychological as well as purely economic reasons for feeling "liquid."[6]

Perhaps more important than the reasons just cited, however, are those provided half whimsically by R. A. Hendrickson;

> Narcotics agents in New York seized a green suitcase containing almost $1 million in crisp packets of new $100 bills from two men who were charged with a conspiracy to distribute heroin. Without cash, what would airline managements use to pay off hijackers ransom demands? How would politicians payoffs be transported secretly to Swiss banks? Would the pushers or hijackers or the conspirators find their game worthwhile if the only medium they had to play with was credit and no cash in bills and coin?[7]

In the same vein, the OECD author previously cited remarked that "one factor that will ensure the continued use of cash is its anonymity, the underground (or black) economy, still less organized crime, could barely exist without it."[8]

Similarly, R. A. Hendrickson, cited earlier, put it this way:

> But why indeed, *if you are not engaged in illegal enterprises*, hold cash that can be lost, stolen, burnt up or otherwise destroyed, which earns you no return and which you find devilishly hard to account for when it is gone? Substitutes for cash in the form of checks, credit cards, charge accounts, travellers' checks and letters of credit are abundantly available, safer than cash and cheaper for large transactions because a cost inherent in using large amounts of cash is the possibility of loss, theft or destruction[9] (author emphasis).

To this litany of negatives, the author should have added the erosion in value of held currency resulting from inflation. (Interest forgone is what economists call the opportunity cost of holding money.)

It should be pointed out, however, that if one anticipates the possibility of a weak currency being exchanged for a strong one—as in the one-to-one exchange recently concluded between the East and West German marks—then it is perfectly rational to hold onto the overvalued currency, but such occasions are quite rare.

Just how much currency is actually held by the public? The data show that on a per capita basis, publicly held currency rose from $179 in 1950 to $1,142 in 1990, an increase of 538 percent. Over the same period, the rate of inflation rose by approximately 440 percent.[10] The assumption here is that there is an excess of currency, over and above what would be necessary to compensate for price level rises. A per capita cash holding in 1990 of $1,079 translates to $4,568 for a household of four. This implies that the average household was holding $4,568 in cash, an amount far exceeding the requirements of daily living. (Even when one considers that a small segment of high earners may hold a disproportionate amount of the cash, the high per capita figure is still impressive.)

In addition, over the past few decades, the US. dollar has become the *de facto* international currency, so that, of necessity, there must be a large amount of currency held by overseas banks and the public. Therefore, the holdings mentioned above are perhaps grossly underestimated.

Herein lies one of the clues to the underground economy, and the economic detectives began to follow the scent. As Shlomo Maital observed, "Like fiscal Sherlock Holmes's, economists search for the underground economy's footprints or fingernail clippings in the guise of excess cash or cash plus checks."[11]

Could it be, these economists cum detectives reasoned, that the quantity of "excess" currency is actually a measure of the amount of underground economic activity? How would one go about measuring "surplus" or "excess" currency in the economy at large? Here we have the genesis of the so-called macroeconomic approach to the measurement of the underground economy.

MONEY SUPPLY: THE PRIMARY SUSPECT

It is as natural for economist to examine the money supply for clues to the underground economy as it is for sleuths to look for the smoking gun. Money, after all, is the main name of the game whether one is dealing with legal or extralegal activities.

At the latest count, there are about thirteen different definitions of the money supply, known to those who follow such things as M_1 to M_{13}[12] the differences among them having to do with degrees of liquidity (how quickly are the various money instruments—bank deposits, C.D.s, mutual fund shares, and the like—accepted as cash, how quickly can they be converted to cash) in descending order. For our purposes, M_1 is the major player. It consists of currency held by the public plus travellers' checks, plus demand deposits, plus NOW accounts. To simplify further, we consider what were historically the main types—currency plus demand deposits. (In fact, NOW accounts and other checkable deposits, like mutual funds, currently exceed the total of demand deposits—but this anticipates the rest of the story.)[13]

Let us look first at currency. There has been, over the last few decades, a change in the denominational composition of the currency supply. Specifically, the change has occurred in the relative growth of large bills. As of September 30, 1990, the single largest denomination consisted of $100 bills, and they comprised over 50 percent of total currency.[14] In an earlier quote, we cited the seizure by drug enforcement agents of a large cache of currency—nearly $1 million in $100 bills. It would appear that the $100 bill is the currency of choice for those engaged in underground activity.

In an excellent study, Michael Carter, an Australian economist, cites a British economist who "noted that larger denomination bank notes have increased at at faster rate than currency as a whole. But the relative increase in higher denomination is much greater than can be explained by the impact of inflation. This, it is argued, is indicative of the expansion of the underground economy."[15] Carter holds, however, that "the major difficulty with this approach is the absence of any convincing rationale as to why underground activity should have any special affinity for large denomination bank notes."[16] Apart from the obvious fact that $100 bills occupy less space in suitcases than smaller denominations do, the evidence for the affinity is largely anecdotal. There was, however, an attempt by an American economist, James Henry, to quantify the amount of large denomination bills used for tax evasion and criminal activities. He concluded that "well over half of the $50, $100, $1,000 and higher denomination bills are held for illegal purposes."[17] (Using 1990 data, the 50 percent formula, yields a figure of about $83 billion in $50-and-over bills.) Depending on what number one chooses for the velocity of circulation, a figure for the underground economy can be derived by multiplication. This is an alternative to other measurement methods using cash as a variable, to be discussed below.

Another personal anecdote may be appropriate at this point. My attempt to elicit from the Property Clerk's Office of the New York Police Department an estimate of the denominational composition of currency sized in drug busts met with failure. The police, I was informed, do in fact record the denomination of the seized currency, but these data are ad hoc and are not totaled or otherwise statistically analyzed.[18]

The conclusion of two Federal Reserve System economists regarding the growth in the $100 bill category, namely that their "theoretical and empirical results suggest that the expansion in the use of hundred dollar bills is related principally to normal economic and institutional forces at work in the above-ground economy"[19] does not contradict the notion that such bills are preferred by those engaged in underground activities. Their findings may be indicative of the fact that underground usage of such bills has increased *pari passu* with normal usage, and there are the further implications that the underground economy is not large and may not be growing at a greater rate than the normal economy—but such inferences may be reading too much into the data. Until contrary evidence surfaces, it is my view that an affinity to the $100 bill does indeed exist. It would be very awkward, indeed, to purchase big ticket items, such as a house, a yacht, a car, and the like, using cash in small denominations.

Not much need be said at this point with respect to demand deposits—the other and larger part of the simple money supply. Demand deposits are funds on deposit against which checks may be drawn, and undoubtedly, such deposits are utilized by firms of all sizes in their everyday business transactions as well as by consumers.

One of the first American economists to investigate the relationship between currency and the total money supply was Philip Cagan, in 1958.[20] He stated that "if we take the 1940 level of the currency ratio, viz. currency divided by the money supply, as roughly normal, currency in circulation in 1945 was 8.1 percent above normal, which implies that there was $10.1 billion excess currency in that year."[21] Cagan believed that large-scale income tax evasion and the hoarding of currency during the World War II years were the cause of the excess. What is important to note here is not the absolute amount of the hidden currency, but the technique that was used, that is, the ratio of currency to total money supply, because with a slight modification, Peter Gutmann used that method to arrive at his startling conclusion about the size of the underground economy in the United States.

Instead of examining the ratio of currency to the total money supply as Cagan did (currency plus demand deposits), Gutmann focused his analysis on the ratio of currency to demand deposits alone. Using the five-year period, 1937–41, as a base and the average ratio of currency to demand deposits that existed then as a kind of normal ratio, Gutmann found that this ratio in 1976 exceeded his normal ratio by some amount (actually by $127 per $1,000 of demand deposits). He attributed this excess currency to underground economic activity and estimated that in 1976, $176 billion of illegal GNP (or 9.4 percent) were generated by this abnormal currency surplus.[22] This was the first time since Cagan that the attempt was made to relate, in a quantitative way, the underground and the aboveground economies. It would be an interesting question to explore the reasons why there was almost a twenty-year hiatus in this kind of research in the United States—but that would take us too far afield. Needless to say, Gutmann's results were quickly taken up by the media, and a great deal of discussion and additional research in this area were stimulated. However, when other economists looked at Gutmann's methodology, a number of vulnerable areas became apparent. The first problem was the choice of the base year period he alluded to. Had a different period been chosen as normal, the ratio of currency to demand deposits would have been different, as too would the ultimate result. The second and perhaps the most telling critique of the method had to do with the reasons for an increase in Gutmann's ratio. Critics pointed out, quite correctly, that the reason the ratio increased was due not so much to the fact of currency increase (the numerator), but to the less than equal increase in demand deposits (the denominator). As Gillian Garcia noted, "No surplus currency has in fact gone to fuel the subterranean economy because there is no surplus currency. The question one should address is where have the missing demand deposits gone?"[23] The answer to this latter question was, in fact, given by Stephen Goldfeld even before the Gutmann-Garcia controversy erupted. Goldfeld noted that there were many new factors on the monetary scene that tended to reduce the relative levels of demand deposits, namely, "NOW accounts, money market mutual funds, savings deposits of businesses and state and local governments, checking accounts at mutual savings banks, automatic investment accounts, telephone [and computer, H. G.] transfers between savings and checking accounts and overdraft privileges."[24] The decline in the use of demand deposits was, in my view, the Achilles' heel of Gutmann's method. There was yet a third weakness that should be noted, and that has to do with the question of whether a dollar of underground money generates an equal amount of gross national product as does a dollar of aboveground money. This is a matter pertaining to the velocity of money—how many times a given dollar turns over, that is, how many transactions in a given time period a dollar fuels. Gutmann assumed that the velocity of an underground and that of an aboveground dollar were equal. None of his critics, to my knowledge, were able to show definitively that Gutmann's assumption in this regard was incorrect. My intuitive view is that the velocity of underground currency is less than its aboveground counterpart, since so much of it is kept in hoards or transferred quickly (laundered) to safe haven banks. In any case, the criticisms of Gutmann's method were basic and, in my opinion, essentially correct. The fact that his overall result (percent of GNP) was arrived at by other researchers using different methods was, in my view, fortuitous. Had Gutmann focused on the increase tin real per capita currency holdings without reference to demand deposits, he would have been far less vulnerable to criticism. Be that as it may, Gutmann deserves credit for opening and stimulating the debate.

BLIND ALLEY—TRY AGAIN

A somewhat different approach to the measurement of underground economic activity was developed by Edgar L. Feige of the University of Wisconsin.[25] Feige reasoned that underground activity is carried on by check as well as by cash; hence, what is needed is a measure that combines both. That measure, according to Feige, is the total amount of transactions in the economy, which he calculated by combining the total volume of demand deposits (times it velocity) with the total volume of currency transactions (times its velocity). The total volume of transactions in a given year is then related to the GNP of that year to provide a transactions-to-GNP ratio. This is a variant of the Cagan and Gutmann approaches in that a base year (or period) is chosen as a reference point—in this case, it was assumed that there was no underground activity in 1939, so the ratio of total transactions to GNP of that year was the norm and deviations from that ratio were ascribed to the underground economy. Feige's method produced results that were more sensational than that of Gutmann's. In 1976, for instance, the transactions method showed an underground economy that was 22 percent of GNP (more than double that of Gutmann) and just two years later, in 1978, the figure rose to 33 percent of GNP.[26]

Moreover, Feige's method gave rise to such anomalies as the finding that the underground economy was negative prior to 1969[27] (this implies, among other things that the IRS was subsidizing the underground economy!) and further, that in 1981 underground activity was as high as 60 percent of GNP.[28]

Commenting on the methods used by Gutmann and Feige, Vito Tanzi of the International Monetary Fund pointed out that their assumptions regarding the nonexistence of underground activity in the base years chosen for comparison (1937–41 for Gutmann and 1939 for Feige) were tenuous, since "after all the era of Prohibition extended into that decade and the New Deal had already sharply increased income taxes. What this means is that, if Feige's and Gutmann's methods were right, the present level of the underground economy in the United States would be sharply higher than their already extraordinary estimates. To this observer, that requires a total suspension of disbelief."[29]

Tanzi, just cited, estimated underground activity by a method that was quite different from that of the other writers but still monetarily based. He assumed that all such activity was determined by the desire to evade taxes. On that premise, he developed a model that predicted with some degree of accuracy, how the demand for currency varied with changes in tax rates. The difference between the demand for currency with existing tax rates and the demand for currency when tax rates were assumed to be zero represented currency that was probably used to fuel underground activity. Tanzi's estimate of underground GNP for 1976 lay in the range of 8.1 percent to 11.7 percent, which, if we average the two, is almost identical to Gutmann's 9.4 percent for that year. One year later in 1981, Tanzi expressed doubt about this 1980 finding: "To accept an understatement (of GNP) exceeding 8 percent, I feel that one would need faith rather than reason."[30]

The most recent attempt to measure the size of the underground economy by indirect means was made by Joel F. Houston of the Federal Reserve Bank of Philadelphia.[31] He used an econometric technique that purportedly enables one to "observe certain causes and indicators of a variable that is unobserved," that is, the level of the underground economy.[32] Since one of the indicators used was that of Tanzi, we include Houston's study together with the previous currency-based approaches, even though additional variables, such as inflation rates, enforcement levels, and others, were included in his model.

Houston's model produced some strange and improbable results. For example, in one year, from 1963 to 1964, the ratio of the underground economy to GNP fell by more than 50 percent. In another case, there was a tripling in this ratio in the period from 1965 to 1969 (+ 214 percent). In 1969, the highest ratio between the entire period 1954 to 1980 was recorded—22 percent. For the end year of this period (1980), the ratio was 15 percent—similar to that calculated by Gutmann's method.[33] There were, however, wide variations from Gutmann in other years: Whereas Gutmann's method showed a 5 percent ratio for 1969, Houston's, as was pointed out above, was 22 percent, and over the period 1965 to 1969, although Houston showed a 214 percent increase, Gutmann's ratio rose from 4 to 5 percent—a 25 percent increase.

Still more controversy—in a 1986 paper, Feige leveled some harsh criticism at Tanzi's methods, stating that necessary dynamic corrections of Tanzi's static method produced "estimates of unreported income and tax revenue losses that are several times larger than those reported by Tanzi."[34]

ON THE WRONG TRAIL?

Where has the trail of the cash taken us? It seemed eminently reasonable to try to arrive at the underground economy via the cash nexus. Though it may be true that not all underground activity is transacted in cash, the bulk of it, in my view, most certainly is, and following that trail was perfectly reasonable. Moreover, as one British economist rather cynically observed, "One might conclude that the monetary approaches are rather easier to apply than other methods. Data on currency and other monetary instruments are readily and cheaply available. All that is needed is a willingness to bash out a few regression equations and as if by magic we have an estimate of the black economy."[35] Although the present writer has considerable sympathy with this view, in all fairness, one must point out that the fact that it may not be difficult to get at the data does not, of course, invalidate the resulting regression equations, which should be evaluated on their merits and on a case-by-case basis. Nevertheless, the rush to the computer does seem to be an endemic disease of the modern researcher. Many of the results of these quantitative labors either could have been predicted beforehand, or they appear to be counterintuitive and the result of a lack of prior reflection on the problem.

Another British economist, Stephen Smith, has pointed out that "only by being very selective about the monetary indicators used and by ignoring those that point to the opposite conclusion is it possible to show any kind of stable pattern of black economy growth emerging from the analysis of cash statistics."[36] The widely different estimates obtained using cash-based data appear to bear out Smith's observation. The earlier British economist cited leveled some additional heavy blasts at the cash sleuths:

> It should be clear from [that] discussion that monetary approaches to estimating the size of the black economy rest upon some rather crucial assumptions that are difficult to justify in practice. It would seem sensible then to treat the estimates obtained by Gutmann, Tanzi and Feige for the size of the black economy in the U.S.A. with a fair degree of skepticism. The margins of error in their predictions appear to be large relative to the estimate, even by the standards of economics, e.g. their estimates could be several hundreds of billions of dollars out.[37]

(Recall Feige's criticism of Tanzi above.) One final shot: "The overwhelming conclusion must be that both the currency demand and transactions approaches suffer from serious defects. Indeed, these problems are so severe that one would be very unwise to place too much relevance upon estimates of the scale of the black economy using these approaches."[38] Stephen Smith is less charitable, his *coup de grace* being: "Estimates of the size of the black economy based on cash indicators are best ignored."[39]

I fear that these criticisms, many of which are well taken, would result in throwing the baby out with the bath water. Certainly, attempts must be made to render the rather broad categories of cash and the even broader one of transactions more precise. Catch-all variables result in a statistical net that is too wide and full of holes, and consequently, not suited to isolate the underground economy variable. It may in the future be possible to arrive at a synthesis of these methods—to develop assumptions that may be generally acceptable so that some convergence in the estimates can be glimpsed. The cash trail, although it has not brought us to our goal of a number (plus or minus a small amount) for the underground economy, is still, in my view, a viable one. Although the cash trail is not altogether a dead end, other trails with perhaps more fruitful clues beckon. We follow one of these trails next.

NOTES

1. "The Effects on Consumers and Creditors of Proposed Ceilings on Credit Card on Interest Rates," Board of Governors of the Federal Reserve System, Staff Study 154, October 1987, p. 6.
2. *New York Times*, April 13, 1991, 50.
3. August Bequar, *The Cashless Society: EFTS at the Crossroads* (New York: John Wiley and Sons, 1981), 125.
4. *The Wall Street Journal*, April 3, 1991, p. B1. *See* also the *New York Times* report on AT&T's Smart Phone, April 17, 1991, D1.
5. J.R.S. Revell, *Banking and Electronic Fund Transfers* (Paris: OECD, 1983), 19.
6. "Americans Hold Increasing Amounts of Cash Despite Inflation and Many Other Drawbacks," *Wall Street Journal*, July 5, 1979, 24. For a more technical explanation of the motives for holding cash, *see* J. M. Keynes, *The General Theory of Unemployment, Interest and Money* (London: McMillan, 1936).
7. Robert A. Hendrickson, *The Cashless Society* (New York: Dodd Mead and Co., 1972), 13.
8. Revell, *Banking*, 12.
9. Hendrickson, *Cashless* 14.
10. *Treasury Bulletin*, March 1991, 137.

11. Shlomo Maital, "Only the Shadow Knows the Underground Economy's Real Size," *Barrons* (November 14, 1983): 16.

12. *See* various issues of the *Federal Reserve Bulletin.*

13. The Economic Report of the President, February 1990 shows the following data for the components of the money supply (M in billions of dollars): currency—$222, travelers' checks—$7.5. demand deposits—281.2, other checkable deposits—286.8, pp. 371 and 372.

14. *Treasury Bulletin* (December 1990): 127.

15. Michael Carter, "The Hidden Economy: What Are the Issues?" Discussion Paper, No. 84, December 1983, The Australian National University, Centre for Economic Policy Research, p. 80.

16. Ibid., 20.

17. James Henry, "Calling in the Big Bills," *Washington Monthly*, (May 1976): 31. $1,000 and higher denomination bills are no longer issued.

18. Telephone conversation with the New York Police Department Property Clerk's Office, March 28, 1991.

19. Richard D. Porter and Amanda S. Bayer, "A Monetary Perspective on Underground Economic Activity in the United States," *Federal Reserve Bulletin* (March 1984): 187.

20. Philip Cagan, "The Demand for Currency Relative to Total Money Supply," Occasional Paper 62, National Bureau of Economic Research, New York, 1958.

21. Ibid., 10.

22. Peter Gutmann, "The Subterranean Economy," *Financial Analysts Journal* (November/December 1977), 27 and following.

23. Gillian Garcia, "The Currency Ratio and the Subterranean Economy," *Financial Analysts Journal* (November/December 1978): 66. *See* also the exchange of letters between Garcia and Gutmann in the *Wall Street Journal*, April 3, 10, and 24, 1978.

24. Stephen Goldfeld, "The Case of the Missing Money," *Brookings Papers on Economic Activity*, No. 3, 1976, Brookings Institution, Washington, D.C., p. 720.

25. Edgar L. Feige, "The Meaning and Measurement of the Underground Economy," Chapter 1 in *The Underground Economies*, ed. Edgar L. Feige (Cambridge University Press, 1989), 13–56.

26. Barry Molefsky, "America's Underground Economy," Report No. 81–181E, Congressional Research Service, The Library of Con-

gress, Washington, D.C., p. CRS-19. In my calculation, I used Feige's revised figures as cited in note 25, p. CRS-18.

27. Molefsky, "America's Underground," p. CRS-19.

28. Carol S. Carson, "The Underground Economy: An Introduction," *Survey of Current Business* 64 (May 1984) Table 2, 29.

29. Vito Tanzi, "Underground Economy and Tax Evasion in the United States: Estimates and Implications" in *The Underground Economy in the United States and Abroad*, ed. Vito Tanzi (Lexington, MA: Lexington Books, D. C. Heath & Co., 1982), 88–89.

30. Tanzi, *Underground Economy*, 117.

31. Joel F. Houston, "Estimating the Size and Implications of the Underground Economy," Working Paper No. 87–9, Research Department, Federal Reserve Bank of Philadelphia, June 1987.

32. Ibid., 3.

33. Ibid., Table 2, p. 15; for calculations using Gutmann's method *See* Molefsky, "America's Underground," Table 2, CRS-15; ratios calculated by the author from entries in the table.

34. Edgar L. Feige, "A Re-Examination of the Underground Economy in the United States," *International Monetary Fund Staff Papers*, 33 December 1986, p. 779.

35. David J. Pyle, *Tax Evasion and the Black Economy* (New York: St. Martin's, 1989), 174.

36. Stephen Smith, *Britain's Shadow Economy* (Oxford: Clarendon Press, 1986), 93.

37. Pyle, *Tax Evasion*, 33.

38. Smith, *Shadow Economy*, 56.

39. Ibid., 108.

3

Tax Evasion and Other Behavioral Clues

THE TRAILS DIVERGE: MACRO VERSUS MICRO

The previous chapters dealt primarily with so-called macroeconomic measures, for example, total currency in circulation, total demand deposits, and total transactions in the economy as a whole. The estimates derived from such attempts at measurement of underground economic activity generate very large numbers. As Derek Blades noted, "The currency/money ratios used by Gutmann and Feige will inevitably result in the inclusion of unproductive illegal activities that have no place in the national accounts."[1] Carol Carson of the Commerce Department's Bureau of Economic Analysis maintained that "monetary methods yield much too high estimates of underground economy."[2] Frank Cowell's view is that "the very large estimates of the underground economy usually depend on techniques of estimation that are not wonderfully robust."[3]

In contrast to the macroeconomic, the microeconomic approach attempts to estimate the size of the underground economy directly through observation of actual behavior in the economy by taxpayers (or tax cheaters), by the spending of households for illegal goods and services, by the activities of so-called informal suppliers, and by sector-by-sector analysis (*See* Chapter 4). Such micromeasures will, almost by definition, produce estimates that are lower than the macrogenerated ones. Depending on the efficiency with which micromeasures are undertaken and their comprehensiveness, a more realistic picture of the underground economy than that obtained by macroanalysis will emerge. It is to such micromeasures that the present and succeeding two chapters are devoted.

THE TAX BEATERS

Consider the following examples of tax beating from a *U.S. News and Report Report* article:[4]

- For a Californian named Molley the approach of the April 17 income tax deadline won't set off the jitters that many people suffer at tax time. The Internal Revenue Service doesn't know about the $550 she earns each month as a licensed professional masseuse. Nor is it aware of the extra $100 or so she brings in monthly from sewing jobs.
- A Georgia mechanic says he fell into underreporting his income after paying taxes faithfully for years. But when he was fired from his job he soon picked up enough auto work to surpass his former income without reporting any to IRS. By the time his unemployment benefits ran out, he says, "I was making as much myself as when I worked for somebody else." He figures that this year he will declare about half his $20,000-plus income and claims to feel no guilt over his tax dodging.
- An Atlanta waiter has been declaring less than half his $13,000 income for the past four years. He's not worried about getting caught, he points out, because there are no records. He reveals only half his tips to his restaurant employer and keeps only small deposits in his bank account. The reason for his rebellion: high tax rates. "I had a clerk job, he explains, and I saw the federal taxes taken out. So I said forget it. I feel I'm contributing my fair share."

- A Washington D.C. cabby for example, estimates that 10 percent of his income goes unreported. "I might get an early morning trip to the airport and not write it down," he says. Another ploy is to report less in tips. The reason? "You know the big guys that make lots of money aren't paying much in taxes."
- . . . a Los Angeles carpet layer began his own business six years ago. Cash payments amounting to about one third of his income went unreported over the years. "Everyone does it," he says, "I thought of it as the expected thing to do."
- "I pay a farmer neighbor $25 to clean snow from my lane," says a Maryland resident. "I'm just one of about 25 customers and I imagine most of us pay cash."
- Says a New York woman who earns $100 to $500 a year on outside editing and writing jobs, "You have to be dumb to pay taxes on the extra income when the government is already taking a third of your pay."
- A craftsman named Gary . . . made $5,000 in six weeks dyeing clothes and selling them to local boutiques. The stores paid cash and the income was left off his tax forms. "I can always think of something to do for money, and most of the time I can do it without telling Uncle Sam."
- Another case is Susan, who pays taxes on the $13,000 she earns as an airline stewardess. But she doesn't report about $9,000 more that she makes from the handwoven items she sells at art fairs and on order.

The numbers mentioned in these reports should be inflated to current price levels by close to 100 percent, in order to obtain a more contemporary picture of the amount of tax evasion involved. Moreover, every reader can undoubtedly supply similar anecdotes from his or her own experience or from secondary knowledge. Each of the cases mentioned represents true "off-the-books" activity—goods or services currently produced that, for the most part, went unrecorded in the National Income and Product Accounts (NIPA), and in every instance, the motive was tax evasion; some cases rationalized by considerations of equity in income distribution. (It should be pointed out here that there is a distinction between tax evasion and tax avoidance. The latter is perfectly legal and is accomplished via loopholes or other characteristics of the tax laws, whereas the former is illegal.) In terms of the prevalence of tax cheating, a survey of 800 Oregon adults "showed that nearly one in four admit they practice evasion."[5]

In the first of a series of hearings on problems of tax compliance and the underground economy, a House Ways and Means Subcommittee met "to discuss findings that about 6 million Americans don't bother to file Federal Income Tax Returns."[6] In his opening remarks, Sam M. Gibbons, chairman of the subcommittee, stated, "We have heard a lot about the underground economy in recent months—the stories about the professional and business people who barter rather than buy, the tradesmen who work a few weeks on the books and a few weeks off, the laid-off factory worker who paints houses while drawing unemployment compensation. We have heard the economists beginning to wonder if there isn't a lot more unreported, unmeasured economic activity than we had ever thought before."[7]

Question: If there were no income taxes (as in that blissful era prior to 1913), would there be an underground economy?

Answer: Yes, there would be. The abuse of drugs, the addiction of gambling, and prostitution are not entirely tax-related.

Comment: The desire to evade taxes (particularly when the marginal tax rates are considered to be high) is, without doubt, a large part of the raison d'être of the underground economy, but not all those who evade taxes should be considered as true undergrounders. Some individuals who do not report all of their income may nevertheless have earned that income in perfectly legitimate ways, which implies that their activity was captured in the GNP accounts. The part not reported represents an involuntary transfer of income from the tax agency to the evader. By the same token, some individuals who do not file tax returns at all may likewise have earned income in legal ways that were recorded in the national accounts—illegal, yes; underground economy, no.

There appears to be some confusion on this point. Philip Mattera, for instance, stated that "the underground economy represents a *shortcoming* in *tax compliance* and may be defined as the amount of *unreported income*"[8] (emphasis in original). The IRS, however, clearly states that "the unreported income estimates should *not* be equated with income earned in the so-called underground economy"[9] (author emphasis). What the IRS does in fact include in its estimates is unreported income earned in the regular economy plus the "legal portion of the underground economy, such as unreported informal supplier income and unreported tip income."[10] Income from what are legislatively defined illegal transactions is specifically excluded from the IRS estimates of unreported income. Such income (for example, from drugs, gambling, and prostitution) is, however, estimated separately by the IRS and other research organizations.[11]

The IRS obtains its estimates from a variety of sources, such as the Taxpayer Compliance Measurement Program (TCMP), which is based on a thorough audit of a 50,000 sample of individual tax returns, and a so-called Exact Match File, which is a merging of household survey and Social Security Administration data and the matching of data filed by employers with those filed by employees.

A partial estimate of the underground economy may be derived by deducting from the IRS estimates income that is unreported from purely legal activities (what we have elsewhere termed involuntary transfers from government to individuals), leaving income from the legal portion of the underground economy (mainly "off-the-books" activity), excluding transfer payments (redistributions via pensions, alimony, and the like), but including undeclared interest, dividend, and royalty payments on the ground that these represent current payments for the use of capital. I would also include rental income undeclared with the legal portion of underground activity. In order to obtain an aggregate number, we must add estimates of income from what the IRS calls, "unreported illegal source incomes" (from drugs, gambling, and prostitution).

We shall attempt such a calculation at the end of the following chapter, where the illegal activities will be explicitly addressed.

For present purposes, let us look at what the data of unreported income from legal-source activities can tell us about the underground economy, both from a one-year look (cross-section analysis) and from multiyear data (time series analysis).

A PARTIAL LIFTING OF THE VEIL—COURTESY OF THE IRS

The single year chosen for analysis here is 1987, for which a considerable amount of detail is provided by the IRS.[12] The selection of items from that year's entries is based on our often repeated definition of the underground economy—that it ought to consist of goods and/or services currently produced that escape detection in our national income accounts.

Tables 3.1 was adapted from a more detailed one showing the gross income tax gap—the amount of income tax owed but not voluntarily paid.

Table 3.1
Estimates of Tax Evasion—1987 ($Billions)

Individual Income Tax	
Underreported Income	
Wages and Salaries	1,417
Interest and Dividends	1,076
Informal Suppliers	7,739
Other non-farm proprietor income	16,646
Farm Income	1,904
Partnership and small business corporation income	3,216
Rents and Royalties	3,141
Non-filers of tax returns (9/10)	6,457
Small Corporation Income Tax (Underreported Income)	2,519
Large Corporations (Assets of $10 million or more (1/2)	7,923
Total	52,038

Source: Adapted from Table 1-1, IRS Publication 7285, March 1988, p. 3.

Table 3.2
Underreported Incomes of Tax Filers, 1987 (Amount Underreported in billions)

Wages and Salaries	9,427
Interest and Dividends (2/3)	8,769
Informal Suppliers	51,417
Other non-farm proprietor income	86,018
Farm proprietor income	11,289
Partnership and small business corporation income	14,589
Rents and Royalties	15,715
Total	197,224

Source: Table 1-2, Reported and Underreported Incomes, Overstated Items and Voluntary Reporting. Percentages for Individual Tax Return Filers, Tax Year, 1987, Income Tax Compliance Research, Gross Tax Gap Estimates and Proportions for 1973–1992, IRS Publication 7285, March 1988, p. 5.

The rationale for selecting the items in the above table is as follows:

- Wages and Salaries—although wages and salaries are subject to withholding at the source, a relatively small proportion may still be underreported and is therefore equivalent to working "off-the-books."
- Interest and Dividends—these items represent a return to capital—a factor of production. (*See*, however, note to Table 3.2)
- Informal Suppliers—these are, in the words of the IRS, "roadside or sidewalk vendors, moonlighting craftsmen or mechanics, unlicensed providers of child or elderly care services and similar operators with informal business styles.
- Other Nonfarm Proprietor Income—mostly self-employed individuals "operating in more conventional ways."
- Farm Income—a portion of farm revenues not reported.
- Partnership and Small Business Corporation Income—a portion of income earned in legal output that is not reported and is hence "off-the-books."

- Rents and Royalties—income underreported arising from the provision of space and from writing activities.
- Nonfilers—individuals who choose not to file at all either because they believe they will not get caught in their tax evasion, or because of forgetfulness or the fact that their income fell below the filing threshold. Ten percent was arbitrarily deducted for the latter case.
- Small Corporations—unreported (assets under $10 million) income from legal output. Overstated deductions were excluded on the grounds that they represent involuntary transfer from the government to the firm. Large Corporations—since the unreported income was not disaggregated, I arbitrarily assigned 50 percent of the reported total to "off-the-books" activities.
- (Excluded from this table were items that could be considered as transfer payments, such as alimony income, taxable unemployment, and Social Security benefits, prizes, and awards. Unfortunately, gambling profits are included in this item, but since they were not listed separately, they could not be accounted for here.)

As can be seen, the total for all of these items was slightly more than $52 billion. One should not be confused as to what the $52 billion represents. It is the amount that should have been paid to IRS but was not. It is not the amount of underground economic activity. To obtain the total income corresponding to the $52 billion, one would need to know the average tax rates for the various categories listed—for individuals, the self-employed, the farmers, and the corporations, assessed according to the tax table for 1987. Presumably, such calculations were performed in order to derive the data for underreported incomes shown in Table 3.2, which was again, adapted from the more detailed table prepared by the IRS.

The rationale for including 2/3 of the Interest and Dividends figure is as follows: Almost all of such income is derived from legitimate business activity, which is either unreported or underreported by the recipient—criminal, but not underground. A portion (arbitrarily chosen) of such income may have been earned via loan sharking or through dividends paid by unregistered enterprises.

We arrive at a total figure of underreported income for 1987 of approximately $200 billion—predicated on the rather heroic assumption that this represents income earned in underground activities. Since this figure is for tax filers only, we must add to it the underreported income of nonfilers. Unfortunately, the IRS did not make such an estimate, so we undertook to approximate it. From the previous table (3.1), it was noted that nonfilers owed some $7 billion in taxes. If we assume an average tax rate of 14 percent the total income corresponding to the said amount of tax liability would be $50 billion. (Average tax rate equals total income tax as a percentage of adjusted gross income. The figure for 1987 was 13.67 percent, which was rounded to 14 percent. *See Statistics of Income (SOI) Bulletin*, Summer 1991 p. 13.) Therefore, the combined total of underreported incomes of filers and nonfilers for 1987 comes roughly to $250 billion.

Added to this total should be the incomes earned in illegal transactions, which we shall postpone for the time being. (As a benchmark teaser, this order of magnitude was about $30 billion in 1976—some eleven years earlier than our data.) Incidentally, the $250 billion figure (excluding illegal transactions) constituted about 7 percent of total income and 5 percent of GNP for 1987. It was also some 2.8 times larger than the total tax gap—a ratio we

Table 3.3
Gross Tax Gaps—Selected Tax Years, 1973–1992

	1973	1976	1979	1982	1985	1986	1987	1988*	1992*
Filers Understated Income	15.4	24.6	36.4	38.1	54.6	60.0	48.3	48.5	62.8
Non-Filers	1.8	2.8	4.5	5.7	7.8	8.1	7.2	7.3	10.2
Corporations	8.8	11.1	15.0	10.7	14.4	15.6	21.4	22.8	31.1
Total	26	38.5	55.9	54.5	76.8	83.7	76.9	78.1	104.1
X 2.8=	72.8	107.8	156.52	152.6	215.04	234.36	215.32	220.08	291.48

Source: Adapted from Table 1.3. Gross Tax Gaps and Voluntary Compliance Ratio, Selected Tax Years, 1973–1992. Same as Table 1.

*Projected

shall employ as a multiplier for the time series comparison in Table 3.3.

For Table 3.3, I extracted and totaled three items from the IRS original—the tax gap for filers, nonfilers, and corporations. The totals for the various years were then multiplied by 2.8—the figure derived earlier from a comparison of total underground income to the tax gap (admittedly a superheroic assumption—but I trust one that will not result in grossly misleading estimates.) There is a difference between the income obtained in Table 3.3 ($215 billion) and that derived from Table 3.2 (filers plus nonfilers) ($250 billion)—a discrepancy of 14 percent. Given the crudeness of both estimates, I am prepared to average the two figures and use $233 billion as the underground income (minus illegal source income) for 1987. Admittedly, averaging two crudes only produces a third crude, which, however, I believe passes the "reasonableness" test. The resulting figures show underground income (minus illegal transactions) rising from $72.8 billion in 1973 to $233 in 1987 (our terminal date), an increase of about 220 percent. Explanation of movement in the series would involve such factors as general economic conditions, changes in tax laws, and changes in IRS enforcement policies—matters that will be discussed in a later chapter.

THE MACRO LEVEL ONCE AGAIN

Is it possible for the amounts spent for the consumption of goods and services (on a national level) to exceed the national income? One way, of course, is that recipients of underground income conceal most of that income but are less likely to conceal what they purchase with it. It is reasonable to expect, therefore, that revealed spending will be greater than unrevealed or partially revealed income. As one economist put it, the expenditure-income discrepancy "relies on the assumption that, although incomes may be concealed or understated, expenditures will eventually show up somewhere. Given that these two concepts should, in principle, be of equal magnitude . . . one can estimate the size of the black economy by looking at the observed discrepancy."[13] This reasoning assumes, among other things, that all or most of the income is spent in the year that it is received, but this may not necessarily be the case. Large amounts of underground income may be spirited overseas, or even deposited in domestic banks or invested in various financial instruments, such as stocks, bonds, certificates of deposit, mutual fund shares, and commercial paper, or the income may be invested in legitimate enterprises, either new or existing. In the latter case, the income would show up in our national accounts as business investment in plant and equipment (capital formation), and not as consumption expenditures. On a national level, spending may (and usually does) exceed income by government borrowing—hence the federal deficit and accumulated debt. Moreover, underground incomes, as has been suggested, may be spent over a period of years. (Many econometric models can be faulted for not taking account of this lag effect in the income variable.)

On an individual or household level, spending can exceed income for a number of reasons: the spending of unrecorded income; by borrowing; by dissaving, that is, dipping into past savings; by liquidating nonmonetary assets; by windfall incomes from inheritance or from lotteries. Consequently, without a detailed knowledge of the sources of income, it would be impossible to attribute the excess of spending over income to underground activity.

Returning to the macrolevel, Carol Carson has pointed out that three estimates prepared for the National Income and Product Accounts are often mistaken as measures of the underground economy. These are: the adjusted gross income gap (the difference between what the IRS and the NIPA statisticians report as income), adjustments for taxpayer misreporting, and the statistical discrepancy. Without going into the details of Dr. Carson's explanation, she effectively demonstrates that none of the three should be used as underground economy measures.[14] In point of fact, the Bureau of Economic Analysis, the agency that develops the NIPA accounts, does not as yet prepare any estimates of the underground economy. The estimate of the underground economy that was derived in the first part of this chapter does not utilize either of the three NIPA estimates mentioned above.

THE MICRO LEVEL: BUYING AND SELLING IN THE UNDERGROUND ECONOMY

If we cannot use the NIPA accounts and if we cannot know all of the sources of income of individuals, what can we do to obtain some indication of underground economic activity on the microlevel (individual or household)? Simple, just ask! Provided that individuals are assured that the information they divulge will never be reported to the authorities, a good deal (but certainly not all) of the information on their interaction with the underground may be learned. Inevitably, biases resulting from problems of nonresponse and false response are endemic to such surveys.

Nevertheless, two researchers undertook just such a household survey "to measure the size of informal activities by measuring the expenditures of households in the informal economy."[15] The method used was a telephone survey of a random sample of 2,100 households. They found that "the earnings of informal suppliers . . . are estimated to have been about $41.8 billion in 1981. This compares to a gross national product of $2,938 billion during the same period. $7.3 billion of this amount was reported on personal income tax returns."[16] The $42 billion (rounded) was 2 percent of personal consumption expenditures for that year, and the $7.3 billion reported on tax returns was 17 percent of earnings—a very low compliance rate. It is most interesting to note that "over 80 percent of those questioned in the survey indicated at least a small purchase from informal suppliers."[17] The kinds of informal suppliers and the amounts purchased from them are shown in Table 3.4.

It should be noted that omitted from this table are purchases of drugs, the service of prostitutes, and the net revenues earned by illegal gamblers and loan sharks—informal suppliers all. In the following chapter, we shall attempt to estimate the amounts in-

Table 3.4
Value of Purchases from Informal Vendors by Type of Goods and Services, 1981 (in Millions of Dollars)

Goods and Services	Amounts Purchased	Percent Distribution
Home Repairs and Additions	12,245	29
Food	9,000	22
Child Care	4,955	12
Domestic Service	3,882	9
Auto Repair	2,810	7
Sidewalk Vendor Goods	1,782	4
Flea Market Goods	1,898	4
Lawn Maintenance	1,447	3
Lessons	933	2
Fuel	749	2
Appliance Repair	744	2
Adult Care	442	1
Cosmetic Services	411	1
Sewing	392	1
Catering	300	1
Total	41,990	100

Source: "Informal Suppliers in the Underground Economy," *Statistics of Income Bulletin* (Summer, 1983): 28.

volved in such illegal purchases and then to complete the above table using those numbers.

That said, it is interesting to observe that 63 percent of the total purchases shown was accounted for by the first three items—home repairs and additions, food, and child care. There are certainly clues here for the IRS to pursue. An intensive auditing of individuals engaged in these activities should produce benefits in terms of taxes recovered, far in excess of the costs involved.

A study similar to the one just cited was done a few years earlier via a survey of 284 households in Detroit.[18] This study focused more on sociological and specifically the ethnological aspects of the "informal sector," and provided additional information on the behavioral aspects of the buyers and sellers. Of interest in this study is the finding that "nearly 25 percent of the services which the respondents purchased with cash were secured through the irregular economy."[19] The authors also found that the most frequent services provided by irregular sources were carpentry, cement work, wiring, babysitting, and painting. The purchase of food, which the earlier study cited as the second most important item, was not mentioned in this study. Surprisingly, "cost was not cited as the most important consideration in choosing irregular producers,"[20] although, "as a whole, respondents did pay less for the services obtained through the irregular economy than through the regular economy."[21]

A conclusion by these authors that bears on our subsequent examination of the labor market is important to note here, namely, "in our research we found little evidence to support popular contentions that the poor, the unemployed, the unskilled and the disadvantaged are actually gainfully employed in the irregular economy."[22]

NOTES

1. OECD Economic Outlook, Occasional Studies, "The Hidden Economy and the National Accounts," OECD Paris, June 1982, p. 29.

2. Carol S. Carson, "The Underground Economy: An Introduction," *Survey of Current Business*, 64 (May 1984): 26.

3. Frank A. Cowell, *Cheating the Government: The Economics of Evasion* (Cambridge, Mass.: The MIT Press, 1990), 197.

4. "How Tax Cheaters Get Away with Billions," *U.S. News and World Report*, March 27, 1978, 102–5; copyright 1978, U.S.N. & W.R.

5. Robert Mason and Lyle D. Calvin, "A Study of Admitted Tax Evasion," *Law and Society Review*, Vol. 12, No. 1 (Fall 1978), 73.

6. "Underground Economy," H. R. Committee on Ways and Means, Subcommittee on Oversight, July 16, 1979.

7. Ibid., 1.

8. Philip Mattera, *Off the Books: The Rise of the Underground Economy* (New York: St. Martin's Press, 1985), 41.

9. "Income Tax Compliance Research," Department of the Treasury, Internal Revenue Service, Publication 7285, March, 1988, p. 1.

10. Ibid., 1.

11. *See* "Estimates of Income Unreported on Individual Income Tax Returns," Department of the Treasury, Internal Revenue Service, Publication 1104, September 1979; also "Unreported Taxable Income from

Selected Illegal Activities" prepared for the Internal Revenue Service by Abt Associates, U.S.G.P.O., September 1984.

12. "Income Tax Compliance," 3.

13. Cowell, *Cheating the Government*, 19.

14. Carson, "The Underground Economy," 109.

15. Kevin F. McRohan and James D. Smith, "Informal Suppliers in the Underground Economy," *Statistics of Income Bulletin* (SOI), (Summer 1983): 28.

16. Ibid.

17. Louis A. Ferman, Louise Berndt, and Elaine Selo, "Analysis of the Irregular Economy: Cash Flows in the Informal Sector," Institute of Labor and Industrial Relations, University of Michigan-Wayne State University, March 1978 (Xerox).

18. Ibid.

19. Ibid., 2–11.

20. Ibid., 2–21.

21. Ibid., 2–22.

22. Louis A. Ferman and Louise Berndt, "The Irregular Economy," in *Can I Have It in Cash*, ed. Stuart Henry, (London: Astragal Books, 1981), 40.

4

Sectoral Clues: The Building Block Approach

THE BUILDING'S FRAMEWORK

One attempt to estimate the size of the underground economy using a sector-by-sector (microeconomic) approach was the pioneering 1979 report of the Internal Revenue Service, to which we have previously referred. This study was followed by a more comprehensive work by Carl Simon and Ann Witte in their seminal 1982 book, *Beating the System*—likewise cited in earlier chapters. Two years after the publication of the Simon and Witte work, Abt Associates undertook a study for the IRS, entitled, "Unreported Taxable Income from Selected Illegal Activities."[1–3]

Most, if not all, of the studies in this area, including the present one, have relied on the three works above-mentioned for basic methodology as well as for bench-mark estimates. Where the present writer differs from the three cited is in the basic definition of what constitutes the underground economy. The IRS study, for example, includes pensions, annuities, and trusts as part of unreported income. This author's view is that these instruments are essentially transfer payments and therefore do not fit a strict national accounting definition of underground economic activity.

In their path-breaking study, Simon and Witte include the theft industry, the fencing industry, and fraud arson as components of the underground. As noted earlier, theft is of the nature of a zero-sum activity that does not result in any additional output and arson actually results in the destruction of goods. (Perhaps the term *deproductive*, to denote the deliberate destruction of goods, might be an appropriate one.) Essentially the same reasoning applies to the Abt Associates study, which includes personal and household theft, employee theft, cargo theft, and Government Program fraud (Medicare, Social Security, AFDC) as part of the underground economy. The Abt study uses legality as the criterion for inclusion, not GNP definitions. The principle that is adhered to throughout the present work is that redistributive activities, for the most part, should not be included in estimates of underground economic activity for the reason that they are not part of GNP.

Chapter 3 utilized the IRS studies for bench-mark data for so-called legal source incomes—mainly "off-the-books" activity. Our task here is to add to those estimates some data on illegal source incomes, that is, from drug trafficking, gambling, prostitution, and the like.

BLOCK NUMBER ONE—DRUGS

An interesting perspective on the drug problem was provided by one writer:

> The inhabitants of the earth spend more money on illegal drugs than they spend on food. More than they spend on housing, clothes, education, medical care or any other product or service, The international narcotics industry is the largest growth industry in the world. Its annual revenues exceed half a trillion dollars—three times the value of all United States currency in circulation, more than the gross national products of all but a half dozen of the major industrialized nations.[4]

Although not completely accurate in all respects, the general thrust of the quotation is well taken. In a similar view, another writer stated that "there were only twenty countries in the world with a Gross National Product in excess of the gross volume of business of the heroin industry in the United States."[5]

How large, in fact, is the illegal drug industry? There are widely differing answers to this query. One observer, for instance, proferred this opinion: "The American illicit drug market, the most lucrative of all markets, produces illicit revenues of an estimated $100 billion in retail sales annually. It is estimated that the American user market consists of about 20 million pot smokers, six million cocaine users and 500,000 users of heroin."[6]

In a 1986 report by the President's Commission on Organized Crime, we find the following statement: "Estimates of the value of the illicit drug trade vary from $27 billion [Abt Associates] to $50–75 billion (confidential analysis performed by several law enforcement agencies and the intelligence community) to $110 billion (House Select Committee on Narcotics Abuse and Control, Annual Report for the year 1984.)"[7]

In all probability, these estimates measure different aspects of the drug trade, leaving us with a conundrum. Since the aforementioned Abt study is based on a careful statistical analysis of the data, unlike some of the anecdotal quotes above, it can be utilized to profile some of the economic characteristics of the three major illicit drugs. Table 4.1 is taken from Abt.

The data in Table 4.1 together with other sources indicate that drug consumption became relatively more important for consum-

Table 4.1
Unreported Illegal Income from Drug Sales

	1973	%	1976	%	1979	%	1982	%
Heroin	2.78	44	3.95	43	5.59	27	6.12	28
Cocaine	2.31	37	3.53	38	9.14	47	9.93	45
Marijuana	1.23	19	1.80	19	5.40	26	6.10	27
Total	6.32	100	9.28	100	20.63	100	22.15	100

Source: *Unreported Taxable Income from Selected Illegal Activities*, Abt Associates, U.S.G.P.O., September 1984, Table 2, p. 62. Percentages calculated.

Table 4.2
Retail Value of Illicit Drugs in the United States

	1988	%	1989	%	1990	%
Cocaine	22.9	44	22.5	45	17.5	43
Heroin	15.8	31	15.5	31	12.3	30
Marijuana	11.1	22	10.0	20	8.8	22
Other Drug	1.8	3	1.8	4	1.8	4
Total	51.6	100	49.8	100	40.4	100

Source: *What America's Users Spend on Illegal Drugs*, Office National Drug Control Policy Technical Paper, June 1991, p. 5.

ers. From 1973 to 1982, income from illegal drug sales rose from $6.32 billion to $22.15 billion, a rise of 250 percent; during the same period, consumer spending for all foods and services increased by 145 percent.[8] Noteworthy, too, is the fact that the product mix of the three drugs changed significantly over this period. Heroin sales, which comprised 44 percent of total sales in 1973, decreased to 28 percent in 1982; cocaine sales, which constituted 37 percent in 1973, rose to 45 percent in 1982, and marijuana, the most widely used drug, which in 1973 was 19 percent of the total, increased to 27 percent by 1982.

In 1991, Abt Associates prepared a study for the Office of National Drug Control Policy in which the data on drug sales were extended to 1990.[9] Table 4.2 is adapted from the Abt study.

Although the headings of these two tables differ somewhat in that Table 4.1 applies to unreported illegal income and Table 4.2 to the retail value of illicit drugs, they are basically similar, since spending by consumers (in Table 4.2) equals (gross) income to sellers (as in Table 4.1). Taking the whole period from 1973 to 1990, drug sales rose from $6.32 billion to $38.6 billion in 1990 (excluding other drugs)—an increase of some 513 percent. Again, relating drug consumption to spending for all foods and services, the latter increased by approximately 337 percent. Looking at the three major drugs, more was spent for them in 1988 than in 1990—a decrease of $11 billion in just two years, a salutary development from the viewpoint of reducing drug consumptions. In absolute terms, spending for cocaine dropped from $22.9 billion in 1988 to

$17.5 billion in 1990; for heroin, the decline went from $15.8 billion to $12.3 billion; for marijuana, sales decreased to $8.8 billion from $11.1.

Of course, the accuracy of the numbers depends on how much is known about quantities consumed of each drug and its average price. As Abt Associates stated: "We offer the $40–$50 billion range as our best estimate given current data. Thus, the range of 40–50 billion is not firm. Data are too sketchy to allow precise measurements. Nevertheless, even if this figure is only approximate, its magnitude is daunting."[10]

Additional data on the size of the drug industry are provided by several reports on international money laundering. One of these, a report prepared by the Group of Seven industrialized countries, "estimated that each year as much as $85 billion was laundered and reinvested from illegal profits from cocaine, heroin and marijuana."[11] Another report by the European Parliament (Strassbourg) stated that "the amount of money laundered in the industrialized world was estimated at more than $120 billion a year. Some 50 to 70 percent of this money was invested in otherwise legitimate businesses."[12]

The rather large sums mentioned in these reports refer to illegal capital flows from many countries and in the latter report, from several sources besides drugs (for example, arms sales). However, in the course of a discussion in the U.S. House of Representatives on a bill that would allow the government to close blanks and savings and loan institutions convicted of laundering drug money (a particularly egregious case that surfaced recently is that of the Bank of Credit and Commerce International), the U.S. Treasury Department estimated that $110 billion in United States cash drug transactions, "continues to be laundered through the world financial system every year."[13] If true, this would imply that the majority of internationally laundered funds originate in the United States. Though indicative of the huge size of the U.S. drug industry, the Treasury figures cannot be used as a datum for one of the building blocks on the underground economy. For one thing, we do not know whether the funds were earned in the year that they were transferred, and for another, some of the funds may have originated elsewhere and then commingled with U.S. funds prior to the laundering process.

Incidentally, to the degree that the fees and commissions earned by the launderers, that is, the banks, S&Ls, the brokerage firms, are not reported to the IRS, they should be considered as part of the underground economy in that financial service is provided. It is extremely difficult even to hazard a guess as to how much is involved.

BLOCK NUMBER TWO—ILLEGAL GAMBLING

> The chance of gain is by every man more or less over-valued and the chance of loss is by most men undervalued.
>
> Adam Smith, *The Wealth of Nations*, Cannan Edition
> Volume 1, p. 120

The propensity to gamble is nowhere set out more succinctly than in the above quote by Adam Smith. Legalized gambling, as in state lotteries and in casinos, generates income for the underwriters—income that in the case of the privately owned casinos is (after skimming) presumably taxed and therefore appears as an entry in our national accounts. We are concerned here, however,

Table 4.3
Estimates of Unreported Illegal Income from Gambling

	1973	%	1976	%	1979	%	1982	%
Numbers	534	34	892	41	1440	49	1915	49
Horses	588	37	713	32	771	26	1025	26
Sports	448	28	571	26	729	25	970	25
Casinos	19	1	19	*	19	*	19	*
Total	1583	100	2195	100	2959	100	3929	100

Source: Same as Table 4.1, Table A-2 p. 112. There is an error in the original table for 1982; the correct total is 3929, not 3454. Percentages calculated.

*Less than 1 percent

with illegal gambling, which is not taxed (but taxable) and which does not appear in our national accounts—that is the service provided by gambling and not its zero-sum effect that is the issue. Here again, we refer to the data derived by Abt Associates as set forth in Table 4.3.

In the original study, this table employs the word "Higher," and indeed these numbers are greater than those reported in an earlier table on page 108 of the Abt publication. The selection of this table is purely arbitrary on my part and stems from my (perhaps naive) belief that respondents to a survey of illegal activity are prone to understate their participation. In any case, these data are "estimates" and are useful for judging trends rather than for hard and fast amounts. The unvarying number for casino gambling, $19 million in each year, appears to be particularly suspect. Given these caveats, the data show that there has been a shift in betting behavior in the case of numbers—from 34 percent of total betting in 1973 to 49 percent in 1982. There has been a decrease in the relative position on horse betting, from 37 percent at the beginning of the period to 26 percent at the end. Betting at illegal casinos appears to be negligible—the legal ones are now where the action is.

Overall, betting rose from $1.58 billion in 1973 to $3.9 billion in 1982, an increase of 148 percent. As indicated above, consumer spending for all goods and services rose some 145 percent over this period, so there has been virtually no change in consumer behavior with respect to wagering.

A statement by R. Mollenhoff, an investigator on the President's Commission on Organized Crime, contradicts a part of the Abt Associates data, indicative of the tenuous nature of the estimates in such areas: It should be noted that among the illegal gambling revenues, sports betting is number one.[14] The data in Table 4.3 show that sports betting is number three, both in absolute and relative terms. Elsewhere in the same report, there is an estimate of $5.03 billion for total illegal gambling for 1983, a surprisingly high 28 percent increase in one year, from the Abt 1982 figure.[15]

BLOCK NUMBER THREE—PROSTITUTION AND PORNOGRAPHY

> I'm not doing anything wrong . . . I'm not hurting anybody and nobody forced me to do this. I do it for the money. I'm a needed service, just like you need to get your hair done.
>
> Rebecca Rand, "best known madam in Minnesota,"
> *New York Times*, May 23, 1991

Prostitution may not be the oldest occupation, but it is certainly the most durable, not having been rendered obsolete by technological change. Simon and Witte define a prostitute "as any person who grants nonmarital sexual access to a number of clients by mutual agreement, and without emotional ties, for remuneration which provides part or all of that person's livelihood."[16] Payment for such services may be in cash, in kind (for example, drugs), in the form of services of one kind or another, or even by credit card!

With the exception of a few counties in rural Nevada, prostitution (the "sex industry" as some prefer to call it) is illegal in the United States. As Helen Reynolds has pointed out, however, "the fact of the illegality makes some of the characteristics of the prostitution industry a bit different, but it does not negate the laws of supply and demand, nor does it make people immune to incentives and disincentives."[17]

Obviously, we cannot rely on household interviews or on periodic censuses to determine the extent of the sex industry. (The latter term is quite broad and should include pornography in all its forms in addition to prostitution.) The difficulty of pinning down the economic characteristics of prostitution was demonstrated in a recent newspaper report:

Turning Tricks Isn't Very Taxing in Italy
Rome (AP)

As far as the tax man is concerned, the oldest profession in the world does not exist in Italy. That was the government's explanation in Parliament yesterday of why prostitutes are not taxed.

"Tax authorities cannot be bound by problems of a moral character," said Stefano De Luca, the government undersecretary of finance. De Luca explained that prostitution is not a recognized profession on tax forms and therefore is not subject to either income or sales taxes.

The New York Post, August 2, 1990

How, then, can we derive estimates of the industry's size for purposes of placing it in our underground economy totals? There have been a number of studies, some based on random interviews, some anecdotal, some biographical, and some autobiographical, about prostitutes. (*See* the Endnotes and Bibliography in Simon and Witte, pp. 262–266.) In addition, a great deal of data are derived from arrest records of prostitutes, but current records may indicate more avid law enforcement arising from political pressures and may not be indicative of either growth or diminution of prostitutes. An example of one of the indirect methods of arriving at estimates of revenue from sales was depicted in the Japanese film, *A Taxing Woman*. The female investigator is shown counting the bed linens as they were taken out through the back door of a brothel to be laundered. Similarly, some Nevada agents used the number of cars parked in the parking lot of a brothel as an indicator of business activity. For purposes of greater accuracy, what one would need to know is the number and types of prostitutes (street walkers, bar girls, call girls), the fee structure, and the number of contacts ("tricks") in order to obtain a figure of gross revenues for the industry. If prostitution were legalized and all sex workers required licenses to work, we would be in a much better position, datawise, but this does not appear to be in the cards for the United States in the immediate future. The AIDS epidemic, however, may be a spur to consideration of such a policy change.

An interesting aside here on the business aspects of the industry is provided by the story of the Mustang Ranch, the first (and only) legalized brothel in the United States to have had a public underwriting of its shares. (Did stockholders become instant pimps?) The ranch was placed into Chapter 7 bankruptcy, and the IRS is attempting to collect $13 million in back taxes from the owners. Whether the enterprise's problems stemmed from a falling off of demand (which would occur either from pricing policies or a change in taste) or from mismanagement, is not clear.[18]

Now to the numbers: Not surprisingly, the estimates of unreported, illegal income from the sex industry are highly varied. Here are some examples, based on a labor force of between 80,000 and 500,000 full-time prostitutes (from Simon and Witte, p. 254):

The prostitution industry contributes between $117 billion and $14.4 billion to the national income of the underground economy.

[Estimate for mid-seventies.]

The gross income of the prostitution industry grossed $2.25 billion a year in the fifties.

The prostitution industry grossed $7 billion to $9 billion in 1970.

The total unreported income of the prostitution industry was $1.1 to $1.6 billion in 1976.

Prostitution is a $10 billion industry. (1978?)

What these very different estimates indicate is that we are not on a very sound footing in this area. Since Abt Associates attempted to proceed in a more rigorous manner than those whose estimates were cited, their compilation of "Net Unreported Illegal Income from Prostitution" merits reproduction here: "1973—$2.6 billion 1976—3.8 billion 1979—6.2 billion 1982—11.6 billion (from Table 4.9 p. 145).

These numbers, according to Abt Associates themselves, are subject to an error of about 50 percent, plus or minus. If we wish to bring the total down to 1990, there are conflicting trends to be considered—first, the inflation factor (about 30 percent) and second, the possible decline in demand. Adjusting for inflation brings the 1982 total to about 15 billion (± 50%).

BLOCK NUMBER FOUR—ILLEGAL ABORTION

Illegal abortion, like prostitution, meets our criteria for inclusion in the underground economy: It is a service that is provided "off-the-books" in contravention of existing law. Data on legal abortions are available and reliable, but those on illegal abortions, for obvious reasons, are conjectural. Thus, prior to the 1973 *Roe v. Wade* decision, it was stated that the number of "illegal abortions could be as low as 200,000 and as high as 1,200,000 a year."[19]

A recent study provides evidence of the declining amounts of illegal abortions: "It has been estimated that nationwide, 84,000 women who could not obtain Medicaid-funded abortions in FY 1978 were able to obtain legal abortions in the private sector, that 14,000 gave birth and that fewer than 3,000 had self-induced or illegal abortions."[20]

Self-induced abortions would not qualify as underground activity, for much the same reasons that we offered for other do-it-yourself activities—more so in this case since little or no purchases of goods from the legal sector were made and no cash at all was generated. Additional, if indirect, evidence of the decline in illegal abortions is shown by the precipitous drop in the number of deaths associated with other than legal abortions.[21] Undoubtedly, illegal abortions are still being performed, but in all probability the numbers are small. Changes in governmental policy, however, that would make it more difficult for women to obtain abortions legally may cause the number of illegal abortions to increase. Even if we multiply the 3,000 figure by a factor of ten and assume that the cost of an illegal abortion is $500, the sums involved would still be relatively small. My own guess is that currently the total unreported income from this source is in the range of $15–$80 million dollars annually. I have included illegal abortion at this juncture more for the sake of completeness than for its quantitative significance.

BLOCK NUMBER FIVE—CHILD PORNOGRAPHY

As in the case of other illegal activities, our knowledge of the extent of child pornography is scanty depending as it does on evidence from police files and other indirect sources. Adult pornography may or may not be legal depending on the conditions under which pornographic materials or services were produced. For example, XXX-rated films and videos are, of course, perfectly legal, but films produced clandestinely in order to evade taxes as well as in contravention of certain regulatory acts, such as the Postal Obscenity and Laundering statutes, are not. There is no firm basis for estimating the revenues from the illegal portions of pornographic activities. There is no question however about child pornography—all of it is illegal under the Federal Child Abuse and Treatment Act of 1974. What is involved is the illegal production and distribution of slides, tapes, video cassettes, films, magazines, and books as well as child prostitution.[22]

With respect to the size of the business, Julia Foreman, writing in the *Vanderbilt Journal of Transnational Law*, stated that "according to a report that the Sexually Exploited Child Unit of the Los Angeles Police Department submitted to the United States Senate, child pornography is an estimated multi-million to a $2 billion yearly industry."[23] For want of more convincing data, we shall assume a figure of $1 billion for the industry.

BLOCK NUMBER SIX—AUDIO, VIDEO, AND SOFTWARE PIRACY

The illegal production and distribution of films, videotapes, audio cassettes, and software piracy have become a huge underground enterprise. As in all the other clandestine activities, estimates are difficult to arrive at. Judging from bits and pieces in newspapers and other media, the loss to the legal firms (excluding tax loss to the Treasury) in the industry is a minimum of $1 billion and probably a lot more.[24] The piracy of proprietary software may properly be viewed in the same light as other thievery, that is, as a zero-sum game. However, when the pirate adapts or modifies a software program he (or she) is engaging in an act of (service) production—hence qualifying as underground activity. Here, too, it is difficult, if not impossible, to provide an estimate of the value of such piracy. That it exists is incontrovertible.

MORE BLOCKS—CIGARETTE SMUGGLING, LOAN SHARKING, BARTERING, AND SKIMMING

In Chapter 2, we placed cigarette smuggling, loan sharking, skimming, bartering, and do-it-yourself projects as marginally affiliated underground activities. The case of illegal gambling, which was also put into the same category, was discussed earlier. What of the others?

As to cigarette smuggling, Simon and Witte provided an estimate of $100 to $200 million as the income earned by the smugglers in 1975.[25] They also indicated that because of the decline in smoking and the convergence of state excise taxes, smuggling activity has probably not increased very much since the 1965–73 days. (*See* also Abt, p. 248) Given, though, the counter trend of increased cigarette prices and the consequent greater incentive to cheat, a figure closer to Simon and Witte's upper bound of $200 million seems reasonable.

The huge range in the estimate of illegal income in the loan sharking business makes one hesitant to say much about it—$300 million to $6.5 billion in the mid-1970s. Deregulation of interest rates, by and large, together with easier access to a wide variety of credit institutions, as well as the vast increase in the use of credit cards, all militate against resort to loan sharking. The industry has probably shrunk, but where it is presently is a puzzle. My guess is that we are dealing with numbers in the $1 to $3 billion dollar range.

On the skimming question: Potentially, the amounts involved in skimming can overshadow any of the activities we have dealt with, including drugs. Consider simply that total retail sales in 1990 were on the order of $1.8 trillion dollars.[26] Even 10 percent of that, a number that many accountants and IRS agents will aver is on the conservative side, yields $129 billion! The sales of large department stores and chain stores should probably be excluded so that small and medium-sized businesses would be the primary loci of skimming.

As was explained earlier (Chapter 2), however, employee skimming simply reduces the profit (hence the tax liability) of the employer and is therefore a type of zero-sum game with both the IRS and the employers as losers. It was further explained that if the employer somehow tells a portion of his output off-the-books, true underground activity ensues. Again the enigma—what proportion of all skimming activity is of the latter kind? I am not prepared to hazard an estimate on this question, so that this building block, which does exist, must be a transparent one.

Our previous analysis of bartering indicated that one should distinguish between the bartering of existing goods and that of newly produced goods and services. In the former case, even though there are tax problems involved, we view it as a zero-sum phenomenon—an exchange of perceived equal values. The latter case is a candidate for underground classification, but since it is virtually impossible to quantify, it is omitted here.

THE HOUSE THAT ESTIMATES BUILT

Presented in Table 4.4 are our estimates of unreported income from the illegal activities discussed in this chapter, being fully aware of the very soft, and sometimes evanescent nature of the "guestimates" on which the dollar amounts were based. The seeming precision of numbers ought not blind us to the nature of their imprecise origins. Nonetheless, here goes:

As a final caveat regarding Table 4.4, it should be noted that the $337.2 billion figure may be regarded as the midpoint of some

Table 4.4
Estimates of Unreported Income from Legal and Illegal Sources, 1990

Activity	Unreported Income	
Drugs	$ 45	billion
Gambling	5	billion
Prostitution	15	billion
Pornography	1	billion
Illegal Abortion	20	million
Audio, and Software Video Piracy	1	billion
Cigarette Smuggling	200	million
Loan Sharking	2	billion
Total Illegal Source Income	69.2	
Total Legal Source Income (see p. 3.a)	268.0	
(1987 Total Adjusted for Inflation)		
GRAND TOTAL	337.2	
Percent of 1990 National Income	7.6%	
Percent of 1990 GNP	6.2%	

range, the breadth of which at this point is unknown. The reader should also be alerted to the fact that the numbers developed here are a product of the definition of the underground economy, which was explained earlier in the present and in prior chapters. Consequently, these amounts may not be strictly comparable with those derived by other writers using alternative concepts. Moreover, the quantities shown here are for one year only; hence, we are not in a position to say anything about its rate of growth, or whether the underground economy as a whole is either increasing or decreasing relative to overall economic activity. It is hoped that others will be stimulated to supply the missing links.

ADDENDUM

The Underground Economy of New York State: A Comment

An interesting and perhaps unique attempt at estimating the size of the underground economy on a state level may be found in a report issued by the New York State Department of Taxation and Finance[27] (hereafter the Report). The Report encompassed legal source activity only. Illegal source income from gambling, prostitution, and drugs was specifically excluded (Introduction). The main areas treated were bartering, interest and dividends, resale and exemption certificates, cash skimming, and independent contractor transactions.

Bartering

In the case of bartering, the focus was on bartering organizations and on tax losses resulting from their operations. The Report points out that a self-employed contractor who engaged in bartering activities would avoid paying the following (page 4):

Federal Income Tax	26%
State Income Tax	10%
Sales Tax	8.25%
New York City Income Tax	3.0%
Self Employment Tax	9.30%
Total Tax Avoided	56.55%

That this amount of tax avoidance is an incentive to engage in bartering activity is self-evident. However, the Report does not distinguish between the bartering of existing goods and services as opposed to those that are newly created. Only the latter constitutes underground activity.

No estimate of actual tax loss is given. The authors state that "the size of the revenue loss associated with bartering is particularly difficult to determine. National estimates of bartering income range as high as $250 billion" (page 4). Insofar as we do not know what part of the bartering transactions represents underground activity as we have defined it and since no source was provided for the rather large estimate of bartering income, no conclusion could reasonably be drawn as to the contribution of bartering to the underground economy of New York State. Nevertheless, the

Report's authors maintain that such an estimate was included in their aggregate figure! (*See* note 10.)

Interest and Dividends

On the question of tax revenue lost because of the nonreporting of interest and dividends, the Report estimates that approximately $150 million of New York State revenues were lost for the 1980 tax year. Apart from interest payments to loan sharks and dividend payments from unregistered enterprises, most such income flows are generated by legal firms producing outputs that are recorded in the national income accounts and are therefore not part of the underground economy as it has been defined. What the actual ratios are between the legal and the illegal flows is difficult, if not impossible, to determine. The revenue loss resulting from the nonreporting of legal source interest and dividend represents an illegal transfer of funds from the state to the nonfiler.

Exemption Certificates

A section of the Report is devoted to Exemption Certificates, which "effectively relieve the purchaser from payments of sales tax at the time of purchase" (page 16). From the perspective of the underground economy, the abuse associated with such certificates represents, again, an illegal transfer of income from the state to the perpetrator: No underground activity is involved, since the goods and services purchased [without sales tax] were recorded as part of the normal economy.

Cash Skimming

According to the Report, "cash skimming and dual record keeping is defined as that activity whereby individuals, either as principals or employees of the same business enterprise, regularly engage in the practice of failing to record legitimate business transactions (as required by tax regulation and proper accounting practice). The cash related to these transactions is diverted to some purpose, business or otherwise, which may escape recording or tax requirements" (page 19). As was indicated earlier, to the extent that goods and services were produced and not recorded, this represents real underground activity. There is no technique for detecting that portion of the skim which represents off-the-books output. On dual bookkeeping, it was stated previously that the difference between the amounts recorded in the two sets of books represents true underground activity. The Report does not cite any figures for the amounts involved in skimming and dual bookkeeping for New York State, although they "are reviewing their own audit history files in order to determine the portion [of the national total] attributable to New York" (page 21).

Nonfilers and Independent Contractors

The Report dealt with the problem of nonfilers and specifically with the self-employed. In terms of size, the authors stated: "Based on estimates developed by the IRS, the Department (of Taxation and Finance, NYS) has estimated that approximately $1.0 billion in income to contractors was unreported in New York State in 1980." Most, if not all, of this income is derived from "off-the-books" production of goods and services, and is consequently part of the underground economy.

Licensing

The section of the Report dealing with licensing discusses the problem of ensuring that all businesses are duly registered, rendering tax compliance more certain. The goal of universal licensing is certainly a desideratum, and it would reduce the incidence of tax evasion, but the goal would be difficult to achieve and would not entirely eliminate such things as skimming and dual record keeping.

As the Report indicates, where there is no withholding of tax at the payment source, such as may be the case with most unsalaried professionals, tax evasion is difficult to detect. For the year 1980, the authors estimated that $3.0 billion of income was un- or underreported by such professionals—true "off-the-book" activity.

Conclusion

The final figure cited in the Report for the underground economy in New York State for 1980 was $25 billion "for all legal and illegal source income" (page 37). This appears to contradict the statement in the Report's introduction to the effect that "criminal" activities were to be excluded. The overall figure is also said to include bartering income, but no such amount is specified. In any case, there is no indication of how the $25 billion figure was derived.

For purposes of comparison with the estimates shown in Chapter 4, the $25 billion statistic, after adjusting for inflation over the decade (roughly 50 percent) comes to $37.5 billion for 1990. Thus, New York State's underground economy, on the questionable assumption that the amount of such activity remained constant, represents about 11 percent of the 1990 national total as derived herein. Given the huge influx of illegal immigrants (many of whom find employment in unregistered sweat shops) and the demonstrable increase in drug trafficking as well as "off-the-books" activity during the 1980s, the 11 percent figure is, in all probability, an underestimate. This writer would place the underground economy relative to the nation's, in the 15–20 percent range—but I hasten to label this as a "guesstimate."

The purpose of this comment was to evaluate the New York effort at estimating its underground economy in the context of the definitions employed in our earlier chapters. Unfortunately, no detail as to the components of the aggregate figure was provided in the Report. However, all efforts by New York as well as by all of the other states should be encouraged. By using a more rigorous definition of what constitutes underground economic activity and one that, it is hoped, will be generally accepted, the states' totals when added may provide yet another route to obtaining an aggregate figure for the United States.

NOTES

1. "Estimates of Income Unreported on Individual Income Tax Returns," IRS Publication 1104, September 1979.

2. Carl P. Simon and Ann D. Witte, *Beating the System: The Underground Economy* (Boston, Mass.: Auburn House Publishing Company, 1982).

3. "Unreported Taxable Income from Selected Illegal Activities," Abt Associates, Inc., Vol. I, Consensual Crimes, U.S.G.P.O., September 1984.

4. James Mills, *The Underground Empire: Where Crime and Governments Embrace* (Garden City: Doubleday, 1986), 3.

5. William J. Chambliss, "The Political Economy of Smack: Opiates, Capitalism and Law," in *Research in Law and Sociology*, vol. 1 (1978): 132.

6. Michael D. Lyman, *Gangland: Drug Trafficking by Organized Criminals* (Springfield, Ill.: C. C. Thomas, 1989), 3.

7. President's Commission on Organized Crime, Report to the President and the Attorney General, "America's Habit: Drug Abuse, Drug Trafficking and Organized Crime," U.S.G.P.O., March 1986, p. 5, note 2.

8. Economic Report of the President, February 1991, p. 286.

9. "What America's Users Spend on Illegal Drugs," Office of National Drug Control Policy Technical Paper, June 1991.

10. Ibid., 43. *See* also, "Annual Report of the Select Committee on Narcotics Abuse and Control," January 3, 1991.

11. *New York Times*, April 20, 1990, D1.

12. *New York Times*, November 26, 1990, D4.

13. *New York Times*, April 26, 1990.

14. President's Commission on Organized Crime, "Organized Crime and Gambling," U.S.G.P.O., June 1985, p. 8.

15. Ibid., 828.

16. Simon and Witte, *Beating the System*, 243.

17. Helen Reynolds, *The Economics of Prostitution* (Springfield, Ill.: Charles C. Thomas, 1986), 4.

18. *See* the articles in the *New York Times*, November 7, 1990, A27 and the *Wall Street Journal*, May 17, 1991, A7A.

19. Frederick S. Jaffe, Barbara Lindheim, and Philip R. Lee, *Abortion Politics* (New York: McGraw Hill Book Co., 1981), 13.

20. *Induced Abortions, A World Review, 1986*, (New York: The Alan Guttmacher Institute, 1986), 43.

21. Ibid. See Figure 16, p. 130 and Table 22, or p. 131.

22. *See* Shirley O'Brien, *Child Pornography* (Dubuque, Iowa: Kendal Hunt Publishing Co., 1983).

23. Julia Foreman, "Can We End the Shame? Recent Multilateral Efforts to Address the World Child Pornography Market," *Vanderbilt Journal of Transnational Law*, v. 23, No. 2, (1990): 439.

24. Tom Bierbaum, "Anti-Piracy Raids on the Rise but They Make Little Impact on $1 Billion Loss," *Variety* (April 4, 1990), p. 37.

25. Simon and Witte, *Beating the System*, 40.

26. *Survey of Current Business* (April 1991), 518.

27. "The Task Force on the Underground Economy," Preliminary Report, June 1982, New York State Department of Taxation and Finance, Processed. I am indebted to Paul C. Rickard, Deputy Director, Public Information Office, New York State Department of Taxation and Finance, for ferreting out what may be one of the last copies of this report—one that was never officially released. Letter to the author, September 12, 1990.

5

Labor Market Clues

WILL THE REAL UNDERGROUND LABOR FORCE STAND UP AND BE COUNTED?

We arrive now at the last of the major paths along which underground economic activity has been pursued. What we hope to achieve by following the present route is to seek an answer to the question of how much and what kinds of labor resources are absorbed in the underground economy, and whether such data provide clues to the size of the underground economy itself. Here again, as in our previous explorations, we are compelled, for obvious reasons, to rely on indirect evidence in an attempt to address these questions. Employees, self-employed workers, or those who are officially unemployed will not voluntarily reveal that they are participants in illegal or criminal activities, or that they are engaged in evading taxes. Likewise, employers who participate in underground activity will not reveal that they are not withholding income taxes from payrolls, that they are not paying Social Security, unemployment insurance, or workmen's compensation taxes, that they may be paying less than minimum wages, that they may be flouting health and safety regulations, that they may be employing illegal aliens or minors, that they are employing workers who are receiving unemployment insurance, disability payments, or Social Security pensions, or that they are receiving AFDC (Aid to Families with Dependent Children) or other kinds of welfare benefits.

In view of these realities, it is no surprising to find that estimates of the number of people employed in the underground economy are as varied as are estimates of the underground economy itself (*See* Chapter 1).

To illustrate, Rafaele De Grazia of the International Labor Office stated (citing Gutmann): "The number of people in clandestine employment in the United States has been assessed at over 25 million."[1] Barry Molefsky of the Library of Congress, however, pointed out that Gutmann's methodology produced a figure of 2.35 million (as of 1978) who "work on a full or part-time basis exclusively in the subterranean sector while they are officially not in the labor force at all."[2] There is obviously something amiss when the same author (Peter Gutmann) is reported as stating in one place that the underground labor force is in the 25 million range and in another that it is slightly over 2 million! Gutmann, himself, in 1985 posited that "25 percent or more of the labor force participates in the subterranean economy. That means 28 million persons, 5–6 million in group 1 [those exclusively engaged in subterranean activities] and 22–23 million in group 2 [those working *subrosa* in the legal economy]" (bracketed text added).[3] (In terms of the 1990 labor force, this formula puts the underground labor force at 31.2 million, with a fifth of those—6.2 million in the core group [1] and 25 million working "off-the-books" in the aboveground economy [2].)

Another writer, Philip Mattera, stated that "a very rough approximation of the underground labor force in the U.S. would be 12 million."[4] He goes on to state that "the figures for off-the-books workers amount to about 10 percent of the official labor force."[5]

Yet another estimate of the size of the underground labor force appeared in a volume of the *Annals of the American Academy of Political and Social Science*: "The measure of labor force participation as an indicator of a nation's economic activity is severely understated if it excludes the estimated one fifth to one third of the population engaged in irregular work."[6] The first part of the sentence refers to the labor force whereas the concluding part refers to population, so it is difficult to know what base the authors have in mind. If it is indeed population, then one-fifth of the current noninstitutional population sixteen years and over comes to 38 million, and at one-third, the number is 63 million! If the reference is to the labor force, then the numbers are 25 million and 42 million, respectively.[7]

In the above examples, what we have is the parable of the blind men touching different parts of the elephant and thus describing the nature of the beast. Undoubtedly, the terms clandestine, subterranean, irregular, and informal encompass different aspects of underground economic activity, so that there is little or no comparability among the estimates.

SOME NOTES ON THE DEMAND AND SUPPLY OF UNDERGROUND LABOR

The extreme segmentation of underground activities has been alluded to many times: Drug traffickers, for instance, have little in common, in terms of their occupational attributes, with farmers who sell their produce at roadside stands. Consequently, it is not possible to develop a general theory that might explain the demand for and supply of labor resources in their sector. The various parts of the underground economy are in the nature of noncompeting groups, although admittedly some overlapping occurs. For example, some prostitutes may become drug pushers and vice versa, though neither competes, generally speaking, with an "off-the-books" plumber or with an illegal farm worker.

One ought to distinguish, too, as Gutmann does, between those workers who are associated with underground activity on a more or less permanent full-time basis and those with only a transient connection—the core and the periphery, as it were. The underground labor force is a dynamic one—it changes with general economic conditions, with changes in tax laws, with law enforcement policies, with demographic and technological developments, and even with environmental situations (for example, AIDS and prostitution). The upshot of all this is that in order to analyze the labor market situation in this sector, one is perforce advised to examine the demand and supply conditions in each of the microlabor markets separately, for example, the demand for and supply of prostitutes, for drugs, for gambling, and the like.

In some cases, a particular activity will be found to be largely demand-driven (crack addicts, for example), whereas in others, there may be a mutual interaction between the demand and supply forces, as is the case when a large supply of a drug appears on the market, causing its price to fall, inducing minors or others with low incomes to initiate purchases. (Why not try it at a nickel a bag?)

WHERE HAVE ALL THE WORKERS GONE?

Information about numbers of workers in the nation comes from two sources: (1) the monthly Current Population Survey (CPS) of the U.S. Bureau of the Census and (2) the Bureau of Labor Statistics (BLS) survey of establishment payrolls. The CPS is the more comprehensive measure and may include workers in the underground economy, whereas the BLS survey is a measure of workers on legal entity payrolls, but even in the latter case, legally employed workers may also engage in underground activities after (or even during) regular working hours. Indeed, many writers (including this one) insist that the case of the simultaneous legal and illegal workers comprises the bulk of the underground labor force. Neither of the two measures, however, is adequate to measure the number of workers engaged primarily in illegal activities, such as drugs, prostitution, gambling, and so forth, nor do they purport to do so. When one considers the independent measurement techniques employed as well as the sampling and nonresponse errors in each of the measures, it is surprising that they differ in absolute terms by about 5 percent and that the long-term trends in the two series are similar.[8] Some writers have assumed that the difference between the two surveys may be used as a measure of the underground economy's labor force, but as Richard McDonald argued, it is highly unlikely that underground workers "would respond in ways that would make the two independent measurements track the same in the long run."[9]

ARE THEY EMPLOYED?

An interviewer for the Current Population Survey (be it a personal or telephone interview) is faced with several questions: Are the interviewees telling the whole truth about who is working or looking for work; are they telling only part of the truth; are they lying altogether, or do they not wish to respond at all? The fact is that we know with confidence the answer to the last question only, that is, the refusal rate, which according to the most recent number stands at 2.4 percent.[10] Why should a household member refuse to cooperate with the CPS? One reason, obviously, is that there is something to hide: Either a household member is engaged in illegal activities (for example, crack pusher), or he or she is receiving some government benefit (AFDC, Social Security, disability payments) that would be terminated if the recipient were working (or not seeking work as in the case of unemployment insurance). Another reason for refusal to participate is general distrust of government bureaucrats. Even though the respondent is told that all replies are confidential, there may still be a lingering doubt—perhaps the Internal Revenue Service may get wind of the fact that taxes are not being paid or not being paid correctly. A strong presumption exists, therefore, that nonparticipation is an indicator of underground activity. This is not to imply that those who do participate in the survey are not engaged in underground activity. It goes without saying that there are strong incentives to prevaricate, because as was indicated above, a large, if not the largest part of underground labor may consist "of on-the-side workers who have a regular job in the aboveground economy."[11]

It should be noted as well that many illegal immigrants, as well as minors who are working underground, will be missed entirely in both surveys. (The perennial question of census undercounting is not relevant as far as the monthly CPS is concerned, but it does matter for the decennial and intercensal population counts.)

WHAT DO THE NUMBERS SHOW?

As is to be expected, much of the writing and debate concerning the underground labor force centers around the data on employment, unemployment, and so-called labor force participation rates—the percent of a given population group that is either employed or unemployed. (The labor force is defined as those over sixteen, who are employed plus those who are unemployed but actively seeking employment. Absent these criteria, the person is declared not to be in the labor force.)

The following three tables are provided as background material against which to evaluate the various hypotheses regarding the labor force in the underground economy. Table 5.1 shows several series: column 1—the civilian labor force; column 2—the numbers employed; column 3—the ratio of those employed to the civilian population; column 4—the labor force divided by the civilian population, the labor force participation rate (hereafter LFPR); and column 5—the numbers unemployed divided by the civilian labor force (the unemployment rate). In Table 5.2, data on the number of self-employed workers are presented as well as their proportion of the civilian labor force. Finally, Table 5.3 shows changes in the labor force participation rates on a disaggregated basis by age, sex, and ethnic group.

Let us begin with Table 5.1. Peter Gutmann used declines in the labor force participation rate as a measure of the underground labor force. He cited, in particular, the drop in this ratio from 1951 to 1976 for males and the 2.1 percent decline for males in the twenty-five to thirty-four year range, as well as the 1.9 percent decline among the thirty-five to forty-four year olds. Based on these data, Gutmann hypothesized that a large percentage of those who dropped out of the labor force went underground.[12] A casual glance at column 4 of Table 5.1 shows, in fact, an almost continuous increase in the labor force participation rate over the twenty-

Table 5.1
Civilian Labor Force and Associated Measures, Selected Years, 1960–90 (in thousands, except ratios)

Year	(1) Civilian Labor Force	(2) Employment	(3) Employment to Population Ratio	(4) Labor Force Participation Rates	(5) Unemployment Rate
1960	69,628	65,778	56.1	59.4	5.5
1970	82,771	78,678	57.4	60.4	4.9
1	84,382	79,367	56.6	60.8	5.9
2	87,034	82,153	57.0	60.4	5.6
3	89,429	85,064	57.8	60.8	4.9
4	91,949	86,794	57.8	61.3	5.6
5	93,775	85,846	56.1	61.2	8.5
6	96,158	88,752	56.8	61.6	7.7
7	99,009	92,017	57.9	62.3	7.1
8	102,251	96,048	59.3	63.8	6.1
9	104,962	98,824	59.9	63.7	5.8
1980	106,940	99,303	59.2	63.8	7.1
1	108,670	100,397	59.0	63.9	7.6
2	110,204	99,526	57.8	64.0	9.7
3	111,550	100,834	57.9	64.0	9.6
4	113,544	105,005	59.5	64.4	7.5
5	115,461	107,150	60.1	64.8	7.2
6	117,834	109,597	60.7	65.3	7.0
7	119,865	112,440	61.5	65.6	6.2
8	121,669	114,968	62.3	65.9	5.5
9	123,869	117,342	63.0	66.5	5.3
1990	124,787	117,914	62.7	66.4	5.5

Source: Economic Report of the President, February 1991, p. 322.

Table 5.2
Self-Employed Workers, Selected Years, 1970-88 (thousands)

Self-Employed Year	Self-Employed Number	Civilian Labor Force	Self-Employed/Civilian Labor Force
1970	7,031	82,771	8.4
1975	7,427	93,775	7.9
1980	8,642	106,940	8.1
1982	8,898	110,204	8.1
1983	9,140	111,550	8.2
1984	9,338	113,544	8.2
1985	9,269	115,461	8.0
1986	9,328	117,834	7.9
1987	9,624	119,865	8.0
1988	9,917	121,669	8.2

Source: U.S. Census Bureau, Statistical Abstract of the U.S., 1990, p. 387 and Table 1, Column 1.

year period from 1970 to 1990—the ratios being 60.4 in 1970 to 66.4 in 1990. Does this imply that the dropouts have returned from the underground? In fairness to Dr. Gutmann, we should point out that the *male* labor force participation rate did, in fact, decline over this period—from 79.7 in 1970 to 76.1 in 1990. The reason that the overall rate increased is due, of course, to the relatively large increase in the *female* rate—from 43.3 in 1970 to 57.5 in 1990.[13] (author emphasis). This raises the immediate question of why we should emphasize the data on males as participants in the underground economy. After all, the workers in so-called cottage industries or in urban sweat shops on an illegal basis are predominantly women, not to mention those engaged in the sex industry.

There are other difficulties with using the labor force participation rate in the manner that Gutmann did. Looking at Table 5.3, we may note that, by far, the largest declines in the labor force participation rate occurred in the fifty-five and over age group for white as well as for black males over the long period 1954–88. Surely, general ill health, disability, and mandatory or voluntary retirement are the salient factors here. We cannot exclude the possibility that retirees would flock to the underground economy, and many do so, but Gutmann's analysis emphasized the prime working age groups. With respect to these groups, the data in Table

Table 5.3
Labor Force Participation Rates Percentage Point Changes, Selected Years, 1954–88

AGE	MEN			WOMEN		
	(1)	(2)	(3)	(1)	(2)	(3)
	White	Black	Hispanic	White	Black	Hispanic
16 +	+8.7	-2.6	+ .5	+23.1	+ 9.3	+5.8
16 to 19	+2.4	-2.5	-4.7	+16.6	+ 5.7	+3.5
20 to 24	+ .3	-3.4	-1.4	+30.5	+ 6.2	+5.7
25 to 34	-2.3	-3.4	+ .1	+40.5	+12.9	+6.9
35 to 44	-2.8	-2.9	0	+35.6	+16.7	+6.8
45 to 54	-5.0	-1.9	-3.2	+29.4	+11.1	+3.4
55 to 64	-21.2	-13.1	-4.8	+14.5	- .6	+6.8
65 +	-23.7	- 9.9	-3.3	- 1.4	- 3.0	+ .8

(1) 1954-88 (2) 1972-88 (3) 1980-88

Source: *Handbook of Labor Statistics*, U.S. Department of Labor, Bulletin 2340, August, 1989, Table 5, pp. 25–30.

5.3 shows that there was actually an increase in the labor force participation rate in the two age groups sixteen to nineteen and twenty to twenty-four for white males from 1954 to 1988. In the case of black males, the data show decreases for every age group in the 1972–88 period. The comment of Levitan and Johnson is apropos at this point: "Until the labor market, most likely in response to government policies, becomes more successful in meeting the needs of black men, it should come as no surprise if growing numbers find preferable alternatives to working in legal labor markets."[14]

The data for Hispanic men show a decrease in the LFPR for the sixteen to nineteen age group, and slight increases in the twenty to twenty-four and twenty-five to thirty-four age groups. However, since these data cover an eight-year period only, 1980–88, they should not be viewed as describing a trend.

Some economists are even skeptical about the use of the LFPR as an indicator of underground labor activity. Co. Hillberger and H. Kuepal, for instance, contend that "changes in work participation rate of the 16 to 64 year olds are predominantly determined by the expansion of the educational system and this factor has no connection with the shadow economy."[15] It then becomes an empirical question to ascertain the numbers of labor force dropouts (or nonparticipants in the first place) who have either returned to school or who tend to prolong their educational pursuits. Intuitively, one would think that those in the younger age groups, that is, sixteen to twenty-five, may be involved in acquiring an education, but this would not apply to the older age groups, where as was noted earlier, disability and early retirement are important factors. However, to maintain, as Hillberger and Kuepal do, that there is no association with the underground labor force over the whole primary working age group is surely an exaggeration.

There is a strong and very reasonable presumption that self-employed workers are prime candidates for underground work. To cite Molefsky again: "Presumably, the self-employed have greater opportunities to hide income and participate in the underground economy than do other workers."[16] How have the numbers of self-employed changed over the years? Table 5.2 provides an answer, with the added caveat that there may be more self-employed than the self-declared self-employed. Be that as it may, the data in Table 5.2 show a rise in self-employed workers from about 7 million in 1970 to approximately 10 million in 1988, an increase of 41 percent over the period. At the same time, however, the civilian labor force rose by about 47 percent, leaving the ratio of self-employed in the labor force at 8.2 percent in 1988 relative to the 8.4 percent in 1970. Apparently, there has been no great movement into the ranks of the self-employed (in relative terms) in the almost two decades covered by Table 5.2. Just what proportion of the 10 million (as of 1988) self-employed are engaged in underground activity is anybody's guess. Some evidence of the extent of such activity is provided by the Internal Revenue Service. Molefsky points out that "an IRS study found that 47 percent of

Table 5.4
Self-Employed by Sector (thousands)

Agriculture	—	1,398
Construction	—	1,427
Trade	—	1,823
Services	—	3,878
Sub-Total	—	8,526
Percent of Self-Employed	—	86

Source: U.S. Census Bureau, Statistical Abstract of the U.S., p. 387 and Table 1, Column 1.

the workers classified as independent contractors did not report any of their earnings for income tax purposes. Twenty-two percent of those independent contractors (who are) considered professional workers, failed to report any of their compensation. These individuals are obviously part of the underground economy."[17]

The Census Bureau has provided a breakdown of the self-employed by sector. Table 5.4 indicates that, as of 1988, the following were the areas of greatest concentration of the self-employed.

Within these sectors of concentration of self-employed, the most important was the general category of services. This statistic is on all four with what we know from other sources of consumer spending for the services of informal vendors (*See* Chapters 1 and 2).

THE EMPLOYMENT-TO-POPULATION RATIO

If, as has been implied by many writers in this field, the underground economy (and presumably those employed in it) is growing faster than the economy as a whole, it follows that the official data on numbers employed may understate the true or real amount of total employment. One would expect, therefore, that the ratio of employment to population would decline over time. This is the reasoning underlying an important article by Edward Denison of the Commerce Department's Bureau of Economic Analysis. The fact is, as Denison pointed out and as the data in Table 5.1

confirm, the employment to population ratio has shown a more or less steady increase over the thirty-year period spanned by the table. That this ratio has not only not decreased, but actually increased,

> strongly suggests that employment is not being increasingly understated. Growth of national income and product is not likely to be understated much as the result of growth of the underground economy unless growth of wages and salaries is understated and any bias in wages and salaries would be matched by a bias in employment. Consequently, the conclusion that growth of employment probably is not being understated carries the implication that growth of national income and product is not being understated much as a result of growth of the underground economy.[18]

Apart from the fact that there are some weak links in this rather long chain of reasoning, one could argue that the employment to population ratios are themselves understated in the sense that they would have shown even greater growth than they did had there not been a large increase in underground labor. Moreover, as has been previously suggested, a portion of those included in the official employment figure is undoubtedly employed n the underground economy. Although the quantity of underground labor cannot be inferred from data such as these, neither can it be concluded from these data alone that underground labor has *not* grown to an extent where national income and product could be affected to a greater degree than envisioned by Denison (author emphasis). The British economist David Pyle observed that "if as seems likely in the U.S.A. most people engaged in black economy work also work in the legitimate economy . . . then a steady or rising employment-population ratio could be entirely consistent with an increasing black economy."[19]

ARE THEY UNEMPLOYED?

The previous section discussed the rate of employment; this one will focus on unemployment. Still in the eye of the storm, Gutmann makes the flat-out charge that "the U.S. official unemployment rate, on which so much government policy depends, is substantially overstated."[20] Clearly, those who are working in the underground economy and have either not responded to the CPS survey or responded that they are unemployed will cause the official unemployment rate to be upwardly biased. If underground workers declared that they are not looking for work for whatever reason, then they were not counted as part of the labor force, and the latter number will then be underestimated. Since the unemployment rate is defined as the ratio of the number unemployed divided by the (civilian) labor force, and since (following Gutmann) the numerator is higher and the denominator is lower than officially measured, it follows that the resulting ratio will be greater than it should be. Gutmann's estimate is that "there is an overstatement of the official unemployment rate of 1.5 percentage points where the official unemployment rate is about six percent. In other words, the real unemployment rate in March of 1979 was 4.2 percent compared to the official unemployment rate of 5.7 percent."[21] Translated into actual numbers, the officially unemployed in 1979 were on the order of 5.98 million, whereas according to Gutmann's analysis, the real number of unemployed was 4.41 million, a difference of over a million and a half workers. In a later essay, Gutmann increased the difference between the official and real unemployment rates to 2.5 percentage points: "When the official rate is 9 1/2 percent the true rate is about 7 percent."[22] The rationale for Gutmann's position is based on what he considers invalid assumptions made by the government counters, namely "(1) that all of the unemployed are full-time unemployed; (2) that all those who say they are unemployed are, in fact, unemployed and not working and (3) that all those who say they are seeking work are, in fact, seeking work rather than not looking for work at all."[23] In response to the second statement, Richard McDonald pointed out that "respondents are *never* asked to directly categorize household members as unemployed."[24] (emphasis in original). It would appear, however, that points one and three retain their validity.

In order to demonstrate that Gutmann's ideas concerning responses are naive, McDonald cites the case of a Washington, D.C. burglar who lived in an expensive house in an exclusive suburb: "What would he [the burglar] have told a CPS interviewer about his labor force status?" McDonald asks, "That he was a burglar. That he was unemployed?"[25] Assuredly, the burglar would not tell the interviewer (if he responded at all) of his profession, but he could lie and say that he was temporarily unemployed, that he was not looking for work and was living high based on inheritance or wise stock market investments, or that he was working part-time. For each of these possible responses, employment, unemployment, and labor force totals would be affected, contrary to McDonald's view that "cover stories to hide the true sources of respondents' incomes could distort the measured distribution of jobs across occupations and industries in the CPS, but would not affect aggregate employment and unemployment levels at all."[26]

The official unemployment rate for 1990 was 5.5 percent, and the total number of civilian unemployed, corresponding to that rate, was 6,874,000.[27] If we assume a 1 percentage point difference between the official and the true rate, that is, 4.5 instead of 5.5, the total number of unemployed comes to 5,615,000 (civilian labor force of 124, 787 times 4.5 percent), a difference of 1.3 million between the two rates. Put in other terms, approximately 19 percent of the officially unemployed are actually employed, or in even cruder terms, almost one out of five unemployed are employed. On the face of it, this conclusion seems a bit much, but based on the arguments advanced by Gutmann and others, which, to this writer have not been countered, it is not implausible to believe that about 1 million workers, at current (1990) levels, are counted as unemployed who, in fact, are working either full- or part-time, and many presumably are employed in the underground economy.

About half of all those who are counted as unemployed collect unemployment insurance benefits and would, on that account, have a strong incentive to conceal their employment. As to the other half, some may have exhausted their benefits, some may be expecting to receive supplementary benefits, and some will have other reasons to declare themselves unemployed, for example, illegal or "off-the-books" involvement. In terms of the total civilian labor force, the 1 million who are the employed unemployed comprise a minuscule amount—less than 1 percent.

ALIENS AND MOONLIGHTERS

In addition to what I shall term the pseudounemployed and the "off-the-books" workers (legally employed or not in the labor force), we should add the category of illegal aliens, who generally are not counted as part of the civilian labor force. A 1980 study by the General Accounting Office (GAO) projected the 1991 illegal population as falling in the range of 9.5 to 13.2 million.[28]

If the ratio of employed to total illegal aliens that prevailed in 1976—about 65 percent—still holds, then the number of illegal aliens currently (1990) employed would be about 7.3 million (the average of 9.5 and 13.2 million multiplied by .65). The GAO study points out, however, that between 64 and 73 percent of such workers paid income taxes, and that between 65 and 88 percent paid Social Security taxes. I would assume, on this basis, that most of these workers are employed in legitimate enterprises, and that no more than 25 percent are working "off-the-books" of legal firms or in other illegal activities. One-quarter of 7.3 million yields 1.8 million undocumented and uncounted alien workers who may be part of the underground labor force.

Much is made in the literature about moonlighting and multiple job holding as presumptive indicators of underground labor. To the extent that we (the Labor Department people) know how many multiple job holders there are—about 5 percent of the civilian labor force[29]—the probability is that the second or even the third job is part of the aboveground economy—otherwise the data would be concealed. Although it can be speculated that part of this group is engaged in "off-the-books" work, my feeling is that the numbers are not significant.

Some researchers in this field write about the potential underground labor force. That is to say, if we add together those who are not participants in the labor force, the total number of unemployed, the total number of self-employed, the total number of illegal immigrants, and those who only work part-time, a maximum or upper bound of an underground labor force can be calculated.[30] Such a calculation, in this writer's view, is virtually meaningless. One can cite innumerable reasons for nonparticipation in the labor force, and ample evidence can be provided for the fact that part-time workers or multiple job holders are, for the most part, not engaged in the underground, because of the fact that the large majority of the unemployed are truly that and most of the self-employed are legitimate entrepreneurs.

PICK A NUMBER

"It is apparent," says Molefsky, " . . . that there is no firm evidence as to the size or characteristics of the underground labor force or whether the official labor force data includes individuals participating in the underground economy. Some portion of the underground labor force is undoubtedly counted. How large a proportion is an open question."[31]

There is, naturally, a great deal of reluctance to set down numbers for entities that are, by definition, amorphous. As De Grazia put it, however, "no serious attempt can be made to discuss such a topic [i.e. clandestine employment] without some, even very approximate, idea of its scale and also because up to the present, there have been practically no texts that give an overall view of the estimate made in different countries."[32]

With full cognizance of the tenuous nature of the estimates that follow, my entries for the size of the underground labor force in the United States for the year 1990, follow in Table 5.5. The 1990 civilian labor force consists roughly of 125 million. Of these, 118 million are employed and about 7 million are unemployed.[33] Following De Grazia,[34] I assume that 10 percent of those employed, namely 12.5 million, are engaged mainly in "off-the-books" activity, and as discussed above, about one-fifth of the unemployed, or 1.4 million, are pseudounemployed for a total of 13.9 million (let us round this to 14 million) of the civilian labor force as being part of the underground labor force. To this must be added those who are engaged in illegal activities, such as drugs, gambling, and prostitution and pornography, who are for the most part not counted as being part of the labor force. I estimate this total to be about 4 million (based in part on the Simon and Witte and Abt Associates work cited above). The third component of underground workers is comprised of illegal immigrants and minors. I estimate this group to be in the 2 million range. A fourth component of the total consists of a portion of the (currently) 25 million retired workers, who presumably are not counted as part of the civilian labor force,[35] and who may be engaged in either legal "off-the-books" work or in illegal activities. Retired workers who are receiving OASDI (Old Age, Survivors and Disability Insurance) pensions may continue to work and earn up to $9,000 annually without losing their benefits. Nevertheless, the lure of earning greater untaxed earnings is ever-present. I am inclined to go along with Gutmann's estimate of 2 percent of the labor force, which at current levels would mean about 2.5million.[36]

Table 5.5
Composition of the Underground Labor Force, 1990

In the civilian labor force — (including 2 million of the self-employed)	14 million
Not in the civilian labor force	
Illicit workers drugs, gambling, prostitution, etc.	4 million
Illegal aliens and minors	2 million
Retired workers	2.5 million
Total	22.5 million

Given the 1990 total labor force (counted and not counted), the underground labor force constitutes some 17 percent (rounded) of all workers in the United States—if the assumptions made here are reasonable.

The estimate of the number of illicit workers may strike some as being unduly conservative, especially in view of the billions of dollars of money flows (*See* Chapter 4) in the drug trade. The rationale here is that the product (drugs) or service (gambling) can generate large money values relative to the numbers employed. Consider, for instance, the five or six people commonly arrested in a drug bust and the many millions of dollars (cash plus inventory) confiscated. Furthermore, to the extent that Mafia-type crime syndicates are involved in the trafficking, the numbers employed, of necessity, are kept small relative to the huge amounts of income produced. Much the same reasoning applies to gambling.

I have indicated, on the basis of rather flimsy evidence as well as on intuition, what I believe to be the quantity of workers engaged in underground economic activity in the United States for one year, 1990. The research task now is to devise more accurate data for that single year as well as to develop a time series, so that we may know whether such activity is increasing or decreasing over time, relative to total economic activity. The challenge is great, but knowing my fellow economists, it will not go unheeded.

NOTES

1. Rafaele De Grazia, "Clandestine Employment," International Labor Office, Geneva, 1984 p. 14.

2. Barry Molefsky, "America's Underground Economy," Congressional Research Service, The Library of Congress, Washington, D.C., Report No. 81-181E, July 28, 1981, p. 27.

3. Peter M. Gutmann, "The Subterranean Economy, Redux," in *The Economics of the Shadow Economy Proceedings of the International Conference on the Economics of the Shadow Economy*, ed. Wulf Gaertner and Alois Wenig (Berlin: Springer-Verlag, 1985), 4.

4. Philip Mattera, *Off the Books, the Rise of the Underground Economy*, (New York: St. Martin's Press, 1985), 136.

5. Ibid.

6. Louis A. Ferman, Stuart Henry, and Michele Hagman, "Issues and Prospects for the Study of Informal Economies: Concepts, Research Strategies and Policy," *Annals of the American Academy of Political and Social Science, "The Informal Economy"* (September 1987): 168.

7. Population and labor force data from, Economic Report of the President, February 1991, p. 322.

8. David O'Neil, "Growth of the Underground Economy, 1950–81. Some Evidence from the Current Population Survey," Joint Economic Committee, December 9, 1983, p. 13 and Richard J. McDonald, "The Underground Economy and BLS Statistical Data," *Monthly Labor Review* (January 1984): 16.
9. McDonald, ibid.
10. Telephone conversation with Demographic Survey Branch of the Census Bureau.
11. O'Neil, "Growth of the Underground Economy," 15.
12. Peter Gutmann, "Are the Unemployed Unemployed?" *Financial Analysts Journal* (September/October 1978).
13. Economic Report of the President, p. 327.
14. S. A. Levitan and Clifford M. Johnson, *Second Thoughts on Work* (Kalamazoo, Mich.: W. E. Upjohn Institute for Employment Research, 1982), 53.
15. C. Hillberger and H. Kuepal, *How Big is the Shadow Economy?* vol. 32 (Amsterdam: European Economic Review, 1988), 971.
16. Molefsky, "America's Underground Economy," p. CR5 25.
17. Ibid., CR5 24.
18. Edward F. Denison, "Is U.S. Growth Understated Because of the Underground Economy? Employment Ratios Suggest Not." *Review of Income and Wealth*, Series 28, No. 1 (March 1982), throughout. It is mildly surprising to find Denison, a quintessential empiricist, resorting to the "much" qualifier several times in the passage cited.
19. David J. Pyle, *Tax Evasion and the Black Economy* (London: Macmillan, 1989), 140.
20. Peter Gutmann, "The Grand Unemployment Illusion," *The Journal of the Institute for Socioeconomic Studies*, vol. 2, No. 2 (Summer, 1979): 22.
21. Ibid., p. 27.
22. Peter Gutmann, "The Subterranean Economy, Redux" in *The Economics of the Shadow Economy*, Proceedings of the International Conference on the Economics of the Shadow Economy, held at the University of Bielfeld, West Germany, October 10–14, 1983. Edited by Wulf Gaertner and Alois Wenig, 1985, p. 6.
23. Gutmann, "Grand Unemployment Illusion," 25.
24. McDonald, "The Underground Economy," 10.
25. Ibid., p. 13.
26. Ibid., p. 13.

27. Economic Report of the President, p. 322.

28. "Illegal Aliens, Estimating Their Impact on the United States," Report to the Congress by the Comptroller General, GAO, March 14, 1980 (processed).

29. *See* De Grazia, "Clandestine Employment," p 16.

30. *See* Rolf Mirus and Roger S. Smith, "Canada's Underground Economy," in ed. Edgar L. Feige *The Underground Economies*, (Cambridge University Press, 1989), 272 and 273; also Philip Mattera, op. cit. p. 136.

31. Molefsky, "America's Underground Economy," CR5 30.

32. De Grazia, "Clandestine Employment," p. 13.

33. Economic Report of the President, p. 322.

34. De Grazia, "Clandestine Employment," p. 14.

35. *Social Security Bulletin* (June 1991): 26.

36. Gutmann, "Are the Unemployed," 7.

6

A Brief Glance at the Underground Economies Abroad

FORENOTE

This chapter intends to provide an overview of the underground economies in some developed and developing countries. The objective is not to present detailed analyses of the derivation of underground economy estimates; rather, this section is included to enable the reader to make some general comparisons between the U.S. case and that of the other countries surveyed. Each country, obviously, has its peculiar institutional structure, which to a large extent shapes the concept as well as the measurement of its own underground economy. It was noted earlier, for instance, that some countries include in their national accounting system what in the United States are considered illegal activities, such as prostitution and gambling. Nevertheless, member countries of the United Nations will tend to measure their economic activity in conformity with the U.N. system of national accounting. At a minimum, therefore, the aggregate of economic activity is, more or less, consistently measured. Now that the U.S. Department of Commerce has decided to emphasize Gross Domestic Product (GDP) in place of the Gross National Product (GNP), which was its

Chart 6.1
Estimates of the Size of the Underground Economies in Selected Countries

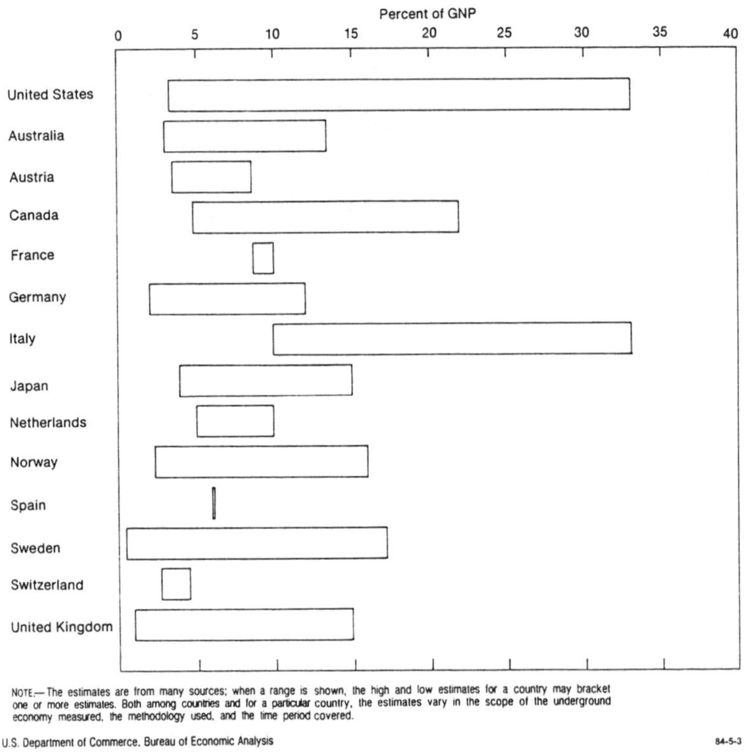

Source: Carol S. Carson, "The Underground Economy: An Introduction," *Survey of Current Business* 64 (May 1984): 33.

previous centerpiece measure, comparisons with other countries will be facilitated.[1] As we shall see, however, the data in Chart 6.1 are shown using GNP calculations, but future comparisons will undoubtedly be made in GDP terms. Whereas the denominator (GNP or GDP) of the underground economy to GNP ratio is, for the most part, consistently measured across countries, the numerator is not. Some of the measures utilize the Gutmann, Feige, or

Tanzi currency techniques (or variations thereof), the advantages and drawbacks of which are discussed in earlier chapters. Still others use the expenditure-income differential or the sector-by-sector approach as in Chapter 4 or the labor market approach of Chapter 5. Needless to say, there is, as yet, no "ideal" measure. Nonetheless, the estimates to be cited were derived by reputable researchers, and they do provide a general indication of the comparison rankings of countries by the relative size of their underground economies. It should be noted that the measures to be shown pertain to time periods prior to 1990, which was our bench-mark year. This implies that, for proper comparison with the United States, the measures should be adjusted for price level changes in the various countries, as well as for the difference in price levels (should there be any) between the underground and the aboveground economies from the given dates to 1990. Price level changes, however, may not be the only factor requiring adjustment—changes in tax laws, in minimum wage, and in Social Security legislation as well as in enforcement policies, all of which can affect underground activity, must also enter the equation. To analyze all of these variables would take us too far a field and, arguably, would absorb the efforts of a think-tankful of researchers. Readers who may be interested in a fuller discussion of such issues as they apply to the several countries should consult the Feige, Tanzi and Bielefeld Conference volumes.[2–4] These caveats noted, I believe that the following material is, for present purposes, a useful overview. Part I deals with the developed economies, and Part II is concerned with the less developed or newly industrialized ones.

PART I—INDUSTRIALIZED NATIONS

An excellent point of departure for this section is Chart 6.1, developed by the Bureau of Economic Analysis of the U.S. Department of Commerce. The comparisons depicted are between the underground economies of the United States and thirteen developing countries. The bars indicate the ranges of the underground economy to GNP ratios (hereafter cited as UE-GNP) for each country as calculated by various measures. Although not strictly correct, the midpoint of each range has been arbitrarily chosen to represent the ratio for each country, and this was done by the not too accurate method of visual interpolation (not having the underlying data). It is quite probable that other eyes may yield numbers that are different from mine, but it is doubtful that the variance will be significant. The purpose of this exercise is to provide an ordinal ranking of the countries by their respective ratios in place of the alphabetical listing in the chart. In descending order, then, from the highest to the lowest ratios, the rankings are as listed in Chart 6.1.

The reader will immediately note that the ratio shown for the United States is far in excess of our own calculation (Chapter 5), the reason being the very high ratio yielded by the Feige transactions approach. However, the point of this listing is not the actual ratios, but the relative standing of the several countries. In all probability, the ratios at the upper bound for each country were calculated by some variant of the monetary method that, as was noted, tends to produce the highest numbers.

The case of Spain is puzzling. It ranks second to the lowest with a ratio of about 5 percent, yet "some estimates suggest that the informal sector may account for as much as a fifth of the Spanish GNP."[5] The latter ratio would place Spain second from the top in our list.

It should also be pointed out that some investigators have found additional intercountry comparisons that are different from those shown above. Hanneman and Frey, in particular, generate a table in which Sweden, for example, with a UE-GNP ratio of 13.8 ranks first of seventeen OECD countries on their list; Italy with an 11.4 ratio ranks fourth, and Japan with 4.1 ratio ranks lowest, as of 1978.[6]

Their results, however, are not in accord with the bulk of the literature on underground economies. Almost always, Italy ranks highest.[7] Another anomaly is the case of Japan—whereas Hanneman and Frey place Japan at the bottom of their list with a 4.1 ratio,

Table 6.1
Country rank by UE-GNP Ratio (Percent)

Rank	Country	Ratio
1.	Italy	22
2.	U.S.	19
3.	Canada	13
4.	Japan	10
5.	France	9
5.	Sweden	9
5.	U.K.	9
6.	Australia	8
6.	Germany	8
7.	Netherlands	7
8.	Austria	6
9.	Spain	5
10.	Switzerland	4

Source: Chart 6.1.

interpolation from Chart 6.1 shows that country to be among the top four of fourteen with a ratio some two and a half times greater than theirs. From our perspective, the most important difference between the Hanneman and Frey listing and that shown in Table 6.1 is the case of the United States, which in their table ranks eleventh out of seventeen, whereas in our view, it ranks second only to Italy. To muddy the waters even further, a 1991 OECD publication stated, "A recent estimate puts the contribution of the black economy in the EEC (European Economic Community) countries as a whole in 1985 at 4 percent of gross domestic product (GDP) with many qualifications as to the methods of its derivation."[8] By way of contrast, the average ratio of the countries on our list is approximately 10 percent—two and a half times the figure just cited.

There seems to be little point in pursuing these differences, which stem from different conceptions and alternative measurement methodologies. Moral: Standardization is sorely needed!

Returning to Table 6.1 (which is viewed as roughly adequate), Italy, the United States, and Canada are shown to have the highest ratios, whereas Austria, Spain, and Switzerland have the lowest. Most of the countries[9] are clustered in the middle ranges, that is, from 7 to 10 percent. Some of the countries with relatively high marginal tax rates (for example, Sweden) are not necessarily found in the highest ranking, and some countries with relatively low tax rates (for example, Italy) are often found at the top. As Michael Carter observed, "No one would deny the importance of taxation in encouraging underground economic activity, but focusing on that factor alone is unlikely to produce either complete diagnosis or appropriate prescription."[10] Among the other factors that influence both the "incentive" and "opportunity" to engage or not to engage in underground activities are: the degree of tax immorality: the labor force participation rate; the unemployment rate; changes in tax burden; the perception of the probability of arrest and the kind of punishment when apprehended. (For the latter point, the work of Susan Long, "The Internal Revenue Service: Measuring Tax Offenses and Enforcement Response; "U.S. Department of Justice, National Institute of Justice, Washington, D.C., 1980, is, for the U.S. case, particularly instructive.)

PART II—DEVELOPING AND NEWLY INDUSTRIALIZED COUNTRIES

As soon as one attempts to investigate the underground economies of the so-called Third World (or developing countries or less developed countries), one inevitably meets the term "informal," which appears to be the term of choice of sociological and anthropological researchers as well as that of the International Labor Office (Geneva).[11]

Referring to the term "informal," Alejandro Portes, Manuel Castells, and Lauren Benton state, "We see no particular difficulty in substituting the term for related ones such as *underground submerged* or *secondary*. Several of the existing chapters employ these terms as synonyms" (emphasis in original).[12] On the same point, Harold Lubell of the OECD in a descriptive paragraph that merits quotation here remarked:

> The underground economy of Western Europe and the United States has a strong family resemblance to the informal sector of the third world. Self-employed builders, carpenters, plumbers and vehicle repairmen start small enterprises that operate outside the tax net, doing business on a cash basis and leaving no accounting records. Garment manufacturing sweat shops produce ready-made clothing for merchant capitalists in apartments and lofts in Paris, Berlin, New York, Miami and other big cities with large immigrant populations. Sub-contractors or larger firms work out of shops in the garages or basements of their homes to minimize capital and operating outlays. Such enterprises usually can accumulate the resources to expand their scale of operation and are convinced that functioning aboveground will be profitable enough to comply with labor and tax regulations. *In this context we define the underground economy to exclude clearly criminal activity such as drugs and prostitution* [emphasis in original].[13]

Depending on how large the criminal sector is in the various countries, one would then have to add some amount to the overall estimate of the informal sector in order to ensure comparability with estimates in which the criminal sector is included. However, when dealing with research in the Third World, one seldom encounters estimates of the informal sector aggregate. The reason is that, more often than not, most of the studies are done by sociologists and anthropologists who tend to take a microeconomic view of the informal economy. That is to say, the focus of the research is usually on a region (for example, Emilia-Romagna of Italy), a city (for example, Bogota of Columbia), or even on a smaller geographic scale, such as that found in the chapter on "Illegal Street Hawking in Hong Kong" in a collection of anthropological studies.[14] Some of the studies have an occupational focus, for example, garment workers, fish peddlers, and the like.

Lest I be misunderstood, I am neither disparaging nor denigrating this type of research, which provides valuable insights into the motivation of participants in the underground economy and illuminates the specific socio-political context in which informal activities take place. Furthermore, attempts to cope with the informal sector must, of necessity, be mounted on an interdisciplinary

Table 6.2
UE-GNP Ratios for Developing Countries

Country	Source	Ratio
Argentina	(1)	40%
Guyana	(2)	7-26%
Peru	(3)	50%
India	(4)	18-21%
Tanzania	(5)	31.4%
Ghana	(6)	32.4%
Israel	(7)	7-15%
Taiwan	(8)	14-30%

Source:

1. "Parallel Economy: Not All Black", Review of the River Plate (Argentina) no. 4253: June 13, 1984, p. 511.
2. Hope, Kempe Ronald "Subterranean Economy in Guyana: the Informal Sector in the Economics Literature." *Caribbean Affairs, (Trinidad)*, (April–June, 1990): 104
3. James L. Rowe, Jr., "Underground Economy Seen Vibrant, Growing", Washington Post (U.S.), October 30, 1983, p. G17
4. K. N. Kabra and N. S. Jagannathan, "Black Money," India International Centre, New Delhi, 1985, p. 34
5. T. L. Maliyamkono and Mboya S. D. Bagachwa, *The Second Economy in Tanzania* (London: J. Curry, 1990), Table 2.5, 147.
6. Ibid.
7. Sam Lehman-Wilzig, "The Charcoal Revolution," *The Jerusalem Post, July* 5, 1991, 14.
8. Sheng-Yi Lee, *Money and Finance in the Economic Development,* of Taiwan (Houndmills, Basingstoke (England): Macmillan, 1990) 37 and 178. (I am indebted to M. A. Turton of the Center for Taiwan International Relations, Washington, D.C. for this reference.)

scale, one which takes full account of the "facts on the ground," so to speak. As was stated at the outset of the present work, the emphasis here is on the economic aspects of the underground economy; hence, I shall not comment on the extensive and very worthwhile literature developed by my fellow social scientists across the methodological "divides."

Table 6.2 presents some UE-GNP ratios for developing countries gleaned from various sources. (Israel is included for convenience, although by all criteria it belongs with the developed group.)

In almost all cases, the ratios in the table are higher than those for the developed countries portrayed in Chart 6.1 and Table 6.2. There are many explanations for the developed-underdeveloped differentials. They can be divided along general and country-specific causes. The general causes for informal or underground activity are embodied in the very terms employed, that is, underdeveloped, less developed, or developing. One can begin with economic stagnation or negligible growth with all that those terms imply: inadequate investment; low consumption levels; weak infrastructure, inadequate banking and credit facilities; chronic unemployment; small-scale decentralized production units (including cottage industry); and hyperinflation. Among the country-specific causes, one may point to such factors as: a non-diversified economy; lack of employment opportunities in the formal sector exacerbated by the migration from rural to urban areas; barriers to the employment of women and/or other minorities; a history of smuggling and of tax evasion; weak institutions for tax collecting and law enforcement; low educational and skill levels; corruption and bribery in high (and low) administrative levels; waste and inefficiency in government (overbloated bureaucracies, as a corollary); political instability; the rigidity and resource allocation in centrally planned economies; extensive cultivation of drug crops. These are some of the salient features that, singly or in clusters, make for large underground sectors. Some of the factors enumerated may well be seen as effects rather than causes of informal activity, whereas others may be mutually reinforcing.

Hernando de Soto's *The Other Path*"[15] is illustrative of the view that informal activities in developing countries should be encouraged by the state on the grounds that they release the entrepreneurial skills and productive energies of people who have been exploited and who are only marginally attached to the normal economy. Informal activities, according to de Soto, result in the production of goods and services that have either not been produced or insufficiently produced (because of monopolistic structures) by the formal sectors and that may be out of the income reach of large sections of the populace. Encouraging informal enterprises, while in the short run depriving the state of tax revenues, in the longer run, by accelerating economic development, will benefit the system as a whole. This writer is in general agreement with de Soto's sentiments.

The other side of the coin, of course, is the fact that many kinds of informal activity result in the exploitation of vulnerable workers who lack the protection of occupational, health and safety codes, who are paid subminimum wages, who may work more than the standard number of hours, and who may not be entitled to unemployment insurance or to Social Security benefits. Given the huge number of workers who attempt at great risk to cross borders illegally in order to obtain jobs such as those just described, one must conclude that the advantages outweigh the disadvantages.

The general rule ought to be that those activities that promote economic development deserve to be encouraged (via subsidies, interest-free loans, enterprise zones, red-tape elimination, and tax abatement), whereas those that tend to inhibit such development should be curtailed or eliminated (drugs, for example). Each case must be decided on its own merits, and in any event, one would expect that a rigid line would be drawn between beneficial and destructive activities when assessing the informal sector.

We should not overlook the fact that enterprises that are the beneficiaries of the state policies noted above thereby leave the shadows and expose themselves to the full light of the economy. Thus the state, in the process of promoting economic development, simultaneously succeeds in diminishing the size of the informal sector.

NOTES

1. *New York Times*, December 5, 1991, D13.

2. Edgar Feige, ed., *The Underground Economies: Tax Evasion and Information Distortion* (Cambridge University Press, 1989).

3. Vito Tanzi, ed. *The Underground Economy in the United States and Abroad* (Lexington, Mass.: Lexington Books, D. C. Heath and Co.)1988.

4. Wulf Gaertner and Alois Wenig, ed. *Economics of the Shadow Economy*, Proceedings of the International Conference held at the University of Bielefeld, West Germany (Berlin: Springer Verlag, 1985).

5. Lauren A. Benton, "Industrial Subcontracting and the Informal Sector: the Politics of Restructuring in the Madrid Electronics Industry," in *The Informal Economy*, ed. Alejandro Portes, Manuel Castells, and Lauren A. Benton (Baltimore and London: The Johns Hopkins University Press, 1989), p. 231.

6. Hannalore Weck-Hanneman and Bruno S. Frey, "Measuring the Shadow Economy: The Case of Switzerland," in the *Economics of the Shadow Economy*, Table 11, 100.

7. W. C. Boeschoten and M.M.G. Fase, *The Volume of Payments and the Informal Economy of the Netherlands, 1965–1988* (Dordrecht: Die Nederlandshe Bank, Martinus Nyhoff, 1984), Table VI-A, 66, shows the ratio for Italy to be the highest by the currency ratio method as well as by the estimates of Contini, Martino, and Forte using other methods. In an article discussing Italy's large national debt, Clyde Haberman of the *New York Times* stated that "the situation would be more tolerable were it not for the Italians' propensity to avoid the tax collector. It has been estimated that if Italian citizens reported all their income, there would be enough tax revenue to eliminate 75 percent of their deficit." *New York Times*, August 2, 1989, D22. *See* also David Pyle, *Tax Evasion and the Black Economy* (London: 1989), Table 3.3, 50.

8. Harold Lubell, "The Informal Sector in the 1980's and 1990's" OECD, Paris 1991, p. 107.

9. *See* Table 6.1.

10. Michael Carter, "The Hidden Economy: What Are the Issues?", Discussion Paper No. 84, The Australian National University, Centre for Economic Research, December 1983, p. 41.

11. Harold Lubell, "The Informal Sector."

12. *The Informal Economy*, 3.

13. Harold Lubell, "The Informal Sector," p. 107.

14. Garcia Clark, ed., *Traders Versus the State:* Anthropological Approaches to Unofficial Economies, (Boulder and London: Westview Press, 1988), Chapters 5 and 6.

15. Hernando de Soto, *The Other Path* (New York: Harper and Row, 1989), throughout.

7

Economic Consequences of the Underground Economy

INFORMATION, MISINFORMATION, AND DISINFORMATION

Question: What if the thermometer reads 104° when the patient's real temperature is 98.6°, and what if the temperature reads 98.6° when the real temperature is 104°?
Answer: Throw the thermometer away.

Critics of the main economic indexes produced by the federal government do not go quite that far, but they come pretty close. Robert Alford and Edgar Feige, for instance, put it this way: "The economic patient is healthy but the social thermometer has gone awry!"[1] Along the same lines, Peter Gutmann observed, "If we don't reexamine statistics and theory, we stand to fool ourselves. Wrong analysis, wrong conclusions, wrong policy prescriptions will be the result."[2]

The reason for these statements is the same in both cases, namely, that indicators such as the Gross National Product, the various price indexes, the unemployment and poverty rates, and productivity measures are according to those authors biased because they do not take into account the existence, size, and importance of the underground economy.

No one seriously denies the existence of the underground economic activity—the question is basically one of size. If the underground economy is 30 percent of GNP, its impact on our economy would be great indeed; if it is only 1 or 2 percent, its impact would be negligible. The estimate derived in Chapter 5 is on the order of 6 to 7 percent, so that although not overwhelming, it cannot be ignored as far as its effect on the economy is concerned. Alford and Feige, however, have an additional agenda in mind. "We shall argue," they say, "that the more important a social indicator becomes as a signalling device for public policy responses, the more likely it is that the indicator itself will degenerate as a descriptive measure of the behavior of the social system."[3] They go even further postulating a conspiratorial, self-serving thesis: "The basic point is that the *internal* incentives within bureaucracies are not likely to lead to a search for the best economic indicators" (author emphasis).[4]

There are some fundamental objections to the Alford and Feige position. First, they undermine their own thesis when they refer to adjustments periodically undertaken to correct the social indicators—adjustments that may arise from improved methodologies, new data, or both. The question arises: Why and under whose auspices were the adjustments undertaken? Why not leave the flawed or uncorrected measure alone, given bureaucratic proclivities? Moreover, even if the bureaucrats desired to leave the uncorrected indicator alone, the search and discovery of the best or better indicators may arise from *outside* the bureaucracies themselves, for example, from legislative oversight committees, from independent researchers, from political opponents, from investigative reporters, or, in the private sector, from shareholder committees or from potential takeover groups (author emphasis). It should also be noted that Feige, in his own research, uses published data on currency, on transactions, on velocity, on price indexes, and so forth—why use adulterated data? Finally, the same authors conclude that "*rational individuals* are basing decision on *irrational information*" (emphasis in original). Presumably, these same rational individuals (not having become irrational) realizing that they were misled by incorrect information will opt to change their decisions based on Abraham Lincoln's aphorism that you can fool some of the people . . . .

This author is not so naive as to deny that pressures on statistical agencies by any given administration (especially at election time) to "cook the books" or "fudge the data" exist, but such instances are few and far between and, in any case, are certain to be picked up by the party out of power, rendering such attempts counterproductive. There are, of course, legitimate differences among scholars at to what a given measure should include or exclude, but such disputes are normal and necessary, and they do not entail any condemnation of the agencies designated to compile the data. Feige maintains that some major economic policy errors were made during the 1970s because:

> the construction of National Income and Product Accounts (NIPA) depends upon tax source data. If tax source data is biased, the nation's basic macroeconomic information system is vulnerable to systematic distortions. This, in turn, suggests that some of the anomalies that plagued the economics profession during the decade of the 1970's might be explicable in terms of distorted official statistics, rather than to explanations of ad hoc shocks to the system or macrotheory gone awry. Could the surprising stagflation of the decade and the unexplained declines in productivity be associated with a growing but hitherto unobserved economy?[5]

Feige's logic is sound, but the factual basis does not support his main argument. It is true, for example, that tax return information is used in the derivation of the NIPA accounts, but such information is used extensively only in some components of the measure; it features less prominently in other components and not at all for some others. In terms of its impact on GNP as a whole, tax data are used in just 4.4 percent of the GNP calculation.[6]

It is therefore extremely doubtful that the biases in tax information given its relatively small impact on the GNP measure could lead to the major policy distortions postulated by Feige. It is quite possible that Feige's alternative suggestion, namely *ad hoc* shocks caused by sharp oil price increases, may provide a better explanation for the stagflation experience of the 1970s. Currently, (early 1990s), the economy is experiencing low rates of inflation and relatively high unemployment rates. Presumably the underground economy is still with us, since according to Feige, it is growing faster than the economy as a whole and represents an even larger part of GNP. Does resort to the underground economy explain both conclusions—stagflation and stagnation—*sans* inflation? Perhaps explain away, rather than explain, is the more appropriate terminology since stagflation and inflation may themselves be statistical artifacts that "ain't necessarily so."

In another essay in the same volume, Robert McGee and Feige state unequivocally that "the growth of the unrecorded sector will produce symptoms of economic decline that are transformed into actual stagflation as a direct result of policy illusion."[7] On the basis of Robert Parker's work just cited, such a view would appear to be a gross exaggeration. This writer is in general agreement with David Pyle's assessment in this regard, namely that "on the whole, the black economy has probably not reached such proportions as either to make macroeconomic information totally meaningless or render macroeconomic policy totally impotent."[8]

There are, however, some aspects of monetary policy that may be affected by the underground economy. It is well known that billions of dollars are transferred overseas making it more difficult to keep track of the U.S. money supply. In a *New York Times* article, Robert Hershey, Jr., stated that "the flow has been so great that the Federal Revenue chairman, Alan Greenspan told Congress last year that perhaps more than half of the U.S. currency is outside the United States."[9] Not all of the currency flow is caused by the underground activity, but a significant amount is largely from the drug trade. Further attempts by the Open Market Committee either to increase or decrease the money supply may be hampered by the fact, as Gutmann quite correctly pointed out, that *sub rosa* funds are unresponsive to changes in interest rates, since much of the money needs to be hidden.[10] The corrective in this case should be similar to the Bureau of Economic Analysis' adjustments to the

NIPA accounts owing to unreporting or underreporting of income. So, too, the Feds should be aware of unobserved funds, and make some shadow corrections in their pursuit of money supply targets or stabilization efforts. Fortunately, given the secular decline in the ratio of currency to GNP, the shadow corrections need not be large.[11]

PROCYCLICAL, COUNTERCYCLICAL, OR CYCLE-NEUTRAL?

Although disagreements persist as to the size of the underground economy, its existence, as noted many times, is not a matter of dispute. It is an economic entity and, as such, is subject to expansions and contractions. An important question in this regard is whether the changes in the size of the underground economy bear some kind of relationship to changes in the economy itself. Given the heterogeneity of the underground economy, one should not expect an unambiguous conclusion. Some components of underground activity may behave as leading, some as lagging, and some as coincident with business fluctuations. Furthermore, even if changes in the underground entity correspond closely to changes in overall economic activity, the relative changes, that is, on a percentage basis, may exacerbate both the upswings and the downswings in the "cycle." One researcher set the problem out as follows:

> If the underground economy is countercyclical, then the underground economy is acting as a hedge to smooth out variations in the reported economy, suggesting that the economy at any given time may be less volatile than it appears. Alternatively, if the underground economy moves procyclically, then it is conceivable that total economic activity may not be as stable as the observed data indicate. While this issue can never be completely settled due to the unobservability of the underground economy, our estimates . . . suggest that the underground economy moves procyclically, indicating that total economic activity is subject to wider swings than the reported economy.[12]

According to this view, the underground economy may be acting as an automatic destabilizer, making it more difficult to implement countercyclical fiscal and monetary policy.

There are, as one might expect, contrary views. Michael O'Higgins cites the work of another economist (Cassell) who maintains that "the development of the shadow economy has not been parallel but contrary to the official economy growth cycle: it is booming whenever the official economy reveals secular stagnation symptoms and vice versa, so that . . . the underground economy is subject to business and growth cycles showing an opposite pattern to that of the official economy."[13] We have then two opposing views: one holding that the underground economy is positively related to general economic activity, and the other maintaining that the underground economy and the formal economy are inversely related. O'Higgins concludes, based on his empirical analysis of the time series date for four countries (Canada, Germany, United Kingdom, United States) that "such consistent and significant results as exist suggest that the sizes of the hidden and formal economies are positively related and, less certainly, the rate of inflation also has a positive relationship. The results for unemployment are weak and inconclusive."[14] The values obtained for the underground economy in the O'Higgins study were derived by the transactions method, which, as previously observed, does not instill great confidence. Both the questionable data and the methodology employed reinforce the notion that it is extremely difficult and tenuous to subject the underground economy to rigorous empirical analysis. Where then can we go from here?

BACK TO THE DRAWING BOARD

Perhaps a fruitful approach would be to examine the major components of the underground economy and using qualitative (read, common sense) reasoning and intuition to try to assess the impact of changing economic conditions on them. For this exercise we may turn to Table 4.4 (p. 65) and examine the individual components listed there.

- Drugs: It is useful to distinguish between addicts and those who are not. Addicts, by definition, have a demand for drugs that is independent of economic conditions (demand in technical terms is inelastic with respect to income and to price). If the addict has a legal source income, that will be used; if not, resort to illegal means will be had. Those who use drugs but who may not be addicted (a questionable proposition) may be influenced by income and price changes as far as their demand is concerned (demand in this case is elastic with respect to income and price). In order to gauge the impact of drug purchases on the economy, one would need to know not only the number of users involved in both groups (addicts and proto-addicts), but also their total expenditures.
  There is something to be said on the other side of the argument, namely, that poor economic conditions will lead many to use drugs as an escape mechanism. If the numbers here are significant, then drug purchases would increase during economic downturns (countercyclical) but not necessarily during upswings (unless a taste for the substance was acquired). Since one would not expect drug purchases to decrease during an upswing, on balance, the cyclical impact is most likely to show a positive correlation.
- Gambling: The view of gambling follows essentially the same reasoning as that for drugs.
- Prostitution: It is necessary to look both at the demand and supply sides of the question. The demand for the services of prostitutes is probably income elastic. That is to say, increases in income will lead to increases in demand (what economists call a "normal" good) and vice versa. However, during periods of high unemployment, many women (and men) may turn to prostitution as a way out. Such an increase in supply may have the effect of lowering prices, and if demand is elastic, spending by clients and the incomes of prostitutes will increase. The net effect in this case is probably a procyclical one.
- Pornography: The demand conditions here, in all probability, render this a procyclical activity.

- Illegal abortion: Demanding this case may increase during downswings if legal abortions for low-income groups are not available; hence, economic behavior would be countercyclical, but since the dollar amounts involved are relatively small, the overall impact is negligible.
- Audio, software, and other types of piracy: A guess here is that demand is elastic, since lower prices are the inducement to purchasers, and since these goods and services constitute a higher percentage in the budgets of higher income groups, the impact in general would be procyclical.
- Cigarette smuggling: Total activity in this instance is highly dependent on the levels of interstate differentials in excise taxes. On balance, activity is probably neutral with respect to changes in aggregate income, but here again, the dollar mounts involved are relatively negligible, and so too its overall impact.
- Loan sharking: Generally, demand for loans from illegal sources would be higher during downswings because of impaired credit ratings and reduced cash flows. Hence, activity in this case would be countercyclical and of some significance overall.
- Legal source income ("off-the-books" activity): There are strong trends and counter trends here. If incomes are at satisfactory levels and growing, the need to engage in such activities would be weak. On the other hand, increases in income may lead to undertakings, such as home improvement, which, other things being equal, lead to the use of "on-the-side" entrepreneurs. Additionally, marginal tax rates that are perceived to be confiscatory will lead to increased "off-the-books" activity. During downswings, the need for income by businesses as well as by workers will lead to increased "off-the-books" activity. The rate of inflation is an independent factor here. High inflation rates, which, absent indexation, push incomes into higher tax brackets, will induce increased efforts at tax evasion. My view is that, on balance, activity in this area is decidedly procyclical, and since sums involved are large, the impact in terms of the cycle is significant.
- It is a foregone conclusion that different readers will disagree with one or all of the formulations presented above, but until better time series for the individual components that comprise the underground

economy are developed, we shall have to rely on (hopefully informed) speculation.

RESOURCE SHIFTS AND ECONOMIC EFFICIENCY

Enough has been written here and elsewhere to demonstrate that the underground economy is not a static, monolithic entity, but that, on the contrary, it is a dynamic one in which resources (labor, capital, entrepreneurial factors) are constantly shifting from the official to the unofficial sectors and vise versa under the impact of changing tax and labor laws, changing technology, changes in societal mores, and business fluctuations. This section hypothesizes on the causes of such resource shifts and their likely direction.

Induced and Autonomous Shifts

It may be useful to distinguish between resource shifts that are induced by tax changes or other specific factors and shifts that occur irrespective of such changes. For example, enactment of high marginal tax rates (say 70, 80, or 90 percent) would most certainly induce a shift of some resources from the taxed sector. Alternatively, with no changes in tax laws, enforcement activity, or regulatory edicts, a resource shift may nevertheless occur in the case of an individual who desires to augment his or her income by pushing drugs or engaging in "off-the-books" work. If someone is occupied full-time in a normal work setting, the decision to perform after-work, off-the-books" (moonlighting), is a decision to substitute work (income) for leisure. Depending on the situation, we may find a complete shift from the formal to the underground, a partial shift or, in the case of previously unemployed resources, no shift per se. Is this kind of hairsplitting worthwhile? It is if one is desirous of gauging the impact of a given change in the economic milieu on underground activities. If, for instance, most of the shifts to the underground are of the autonomous rather than the induced kind, changes in tax laws may not appreciably affect that activity.

What are the consequences of resource shifts on the overall efficiency of our productive machine? One economist answered this query as follows: "Largely ignored have been the effects of the underground economy on the efficiency of resource use. The existence of a sector to which resources may move to evade taxation means that taxes drive a wedge between the returns to factors in different sectors and so create an inefficiency or welfare cost."[15] To paraphrase, what this economist is saying is that shifts in resources that are not determined by cost and efficiency considerations, but are in a sense artificially induced, entail efficiency losses in the system. There is a corollary that should be pointed out in this context, that is, that generally access to credit in the underground economy is, for obvious reasons, restricted. This factor, together with security considerations, implies a deficiency in capital use and, in turn, the implication that output per unit of input (productivity) will be lower in the underground than in the official economy.

TAX CUTS AND THEIR EFFECTS

Differing views on the effect of tax cuts on the underground economy may well be the result of overlooking the distinction made earlier between induced and autonomous resource shifts.

To illustrate, Robert M. Bleiberg writing in *Barrons* stated emphatically that "a systematic lowering of the tax burden would lessen the temptation to operate in the shadows, thereby shifting production and trade to the above-ground [and taxable] economy."[16] This would be true of course only for those activities that are of the induced type and would not affect the autonomously determined shifts. One accountant went so far as to say that "once people learned how to evade 70 percent taxes, they would continue to evade at 50 percent."[17] In the same article, there was a citation from an American Bar Association report to the effect that lowered tax rates did not increase the proportion of Americans who file taxes."[18]

Nevertheless, there is general agreement in the literature that high marginal tax rates do generate incentives to tax evasion, but tax evasion per se does not necessarily imply that resources are shifting to the underground. There are numerous techniques for evading taxes, such as skimming, shifting funds abroad to tax havens, overstating expenses, and the like, but none of these methods results in an actual shift of real, as opposed to financial, resources underground. All undergrounders are tax evaders, but not all tax evaders are undergrounders.

A rapid rise in the price level (inflation) will, as we have noted, cause an increase in tax evasion and may, in some cases, also induce a resource shift to the underground. If the prices of various goods and services rise rapidly, people will seek alternative, less costly substitutes, and these may be available from underground sources. The flourishing black market in the former Soviet Union is a contemporary illustration of this phenomenon.

Some practitioners of the "dismal science," are strange as it may seem optimists and can even discern some benefits from tax evasion! For example, "some Italian economists argue that a measure of tax evasion is healthy, for it gives people money to pay for private schools, messengers and facsimile machines that are increasingly needed as alternatives to the hopeless public services."[19] More to the point, "tax evasion is not necessarily a bad thing, at least economically speaking . . . .It has been pointed out . . . that the loss to the tax authorities may be more apparent than real if the alternative to tax evasion is not payment but a shift of activity which leads to a reduction in revenue. Thus, suppression of evasion may lead to a loss to all parties."[20] Also, David Pyle queried, "Should we worry about tax evasion or does it serve a useful social function, for example, in providing employment that would otherwise not exist."[21] The underground economy is viewed here as a kind of safety valve, the absence of which may cause social tensions and eruptions.

There is an important consideration regarding a lowering of marginal tax rates in order to stem tax evasion that should not be overlooked, namely, that reducing high marginal tax rates (whatever the economic justification in terms of stimulating investment) has the effect of diminishing the progressivity of the tax schedule, thereby skewing the after-tax income distribution further away from equality.

Returning to the question of the efficacy of tax cuts as it relates to the underground economy. Michael O'Higgins' view is that:

> On a wider canvas, the results suggest that insofar as the hidden economy has grown in recent years such growth is more related to factors of a long-term nature, than to fluctuations in economic performance. The hidden economy may, therefore be a function not of cyclical [*See* the discussion above, author] but of structural changes in the measured economy . . . .If it were true . . . it would suggest that any growth in the hidden economy would not necessarily be stopped by the familiar prescription of cuts in taxes or income maintenance benefits."[22]

O'Higgins is suggesting that underground activity may, in fact, be due to long-term, autonomous shifts in resource use, but an analysis of what the nature of such shifts may be and their etiology is not provided.

REVENUE LOSS AND ITS CONSEQUENCE

At was noted above, all underground activities result in tax evasion (at least before the income is spent). Therefore, at the outset, there is a loss to the treasury. One should not, in addition, overlook the cost of law enforcement, which adds significantly to governmental outlays and which, together with the initial tax loss, serves to exacerbate the deficit (or to reduce a surplus). In an effort to compensate for the diminished tax base as well as the reduced revenues (and in the absence of reduced government expenditures), taxes will be increased. The increase in (especially marginal) taxes may induce a resource shift to the underground—thus generating a vicious cycle. Moreover, increased taxes have the effect of reducing investment and savings, and thus inhibiting economic growth. Obviously, this worst-case scenario will not materialize if the revenue shortfall is not relatively large. Given the estimate of the underground economy developed in Chapter 4 of approximately $350 billion (rounded) for 1990, the amount of taxes that have been evaded can be calculated by using an average tax rate for that year of about 14 percent[23]—yielding a (rounded) sum of about $50 billion, representing the amount of taxes that would have been collected had there been no underground economy. Subtracting the evaded $50 billion from the $220 billion deficit for 1990 means that the deficit would instead have been $170 billion or, alternatively, the evaded taxes would have constituted approximately 23 percent of the deficit.

To the extent that some of the underground goods and services (the "goods" not the "bads") would not have been produced at all (for example, lumber may not have been purchased for that house extension paid for in undeclared cash) in the regular economy, a partial offset should be taken; that is to say, the total income in the ratio of taxes paid to income would be higher and the average tax rate correspondingly lower.

TAX MORALITY

One often-quoted study found that nearly one out of every four persons admitted to some kind of income tax evasion.[24] Frank Cowell has pointed out that a person's propensity to dodge taxes seems to be strongly affected by the number of other people who are already doing the same."[25] This kind of crowd instinct can lead to what Cowell has termed the "paradox of tax evasion"—"if all do it and the production of public goods falls, all will be worse off."[26] The decline in voluntary compliance on which the U.S. tax system is predicated may be of far greater consequence than the tax evaded sums involved, for if one aspect of the social contract may be abrogated, other kinds may well follow.

ILLUMINATING THE SHADOWS

Although an attempt has been made to place the underground economy in perspective—not something to be unduly alarmed about, but not something to sweep under the rug either—it is nonetheless of interest to inquire about what options ought to be pursued in order to diminish its extent and to control its spread.

Peter Gutmann advocates a carrot and stick approach: "Use of the carrot to draw people back into the regular economy requires a reduction in the presently substantial financial incentives to operate in the subterranean economy. Use of the stick requires an increase in the likelihood of apprehension by the authorities and increased penalties for tax evasion."[27] There can be no quarrel with this general approach—how to implement the recommendations is the difficult part. Some equity problems associated with lowering marginal tax rates (the carrot) have already been indicated. Eliminating governmental regulations (another carrot), which encourage *sub rosa* activity, must be carefully examined on a case-by-case basis, especially if the regulations may involve health, safety, and environmental concerns. How shall we handle illegal activities, such as drugs, gambling, and prostitution? Steps to legalize gambling (more carrot) have already been taken via state lotteries, Off Track Betting parlors, and gambling casinos—as one writer remarked "thus putting gambling money into the public treasury rather than into the pockets of organized criminals."[28] Questions to be raised here are: (1) whether legalized gambling has created more gamblers, (2) how to prevent skimming and money laundering in such a cash milieu, and (3) how to ensure that organized crime is not involved.

Donald Cressey also suggested that "the profits going to organized criminals from usury would be greatly reduced if a governmental agency went into competition with usurers [a stick] providing short-term loans for desperate persons who have no collateral except their bodies. Universities and government agencies already provide such loans to needy students."[29] For one thing, student loans are not short term, and for another, governmental agencies may be competing with banks or finance companies, which may wish to be in the same business.

Dealing with the drug problem is a daunting task. Many have suggested decriminalization, if not outright legalization. Thomas

Schelling, for instance, is of the opinion that "if narcotics were not illegal there could be no black market and no monopoly profits; the interest in 'pushing' it would not be much greater than the pharmaceutical interest in pills to reduce the symptoms of common colds."[30] The problem with this view is that if addiction sets in, "pushing" would not be necessary; rather the situation would be a demand-driven one. On this point, Mark Moore stated, "The single, most important objective of narcotics enforcement strategy is to discourage people who are not now using heroin from the beginning to do so."[31] This is not to deny the necessity for surveillance, interdiction, and other such strategies.

The temptation on the part of some quarters to legalize at least some drugs is understandable, though not necessarily justifiable. For instance, "In the U.S. the *Boston Business Journal* and *Wall Street Journal* have been discussing how much tax the federal government could make out of the (Cannabis) trade if legalized. $5–$10 billion per annum are the current estimates."[32] The costs in terms of lost output, and of direct and indirect medical costs attributable to drug use would surely be an offset to those estimates.

An important caveat should be noted here; comparisons with the experience of other countries with legalization of drugs (Netherlands, United Kingdom, Sweden), although illuminating, are not necessarily convincing. The demographic, geographic, and institutional milieux in the United States are too disparate relative to other countries for such analogies to be applicable.

Arguments for the legalization of prostitution are almost as old as the occupation itself—to cite one example, "State control would provide a double economy in that by bringing prostitution into the regular, formal economy it would provide an opportunity for the state to benefit through taxation from the profits of prostitution while removing the costs of police and court time."[33]

Omitted from this quote are the health aspects of prostitution. In countries where prostitution is legal, practitioners are required to undergo monthly health checkups and are not permitted to work unless they are certified by a physician to be free of disease. This aspect of the problem is of crucial importance because of the worldwide AIDS epidemic. Prostitution is sometimes characterized as a victimless crime, but both the prostitute and the client may now be victims of (so far) dreaded and intractable sexually transmitted diseases. It is for this reason, more than any others, that the present writer is now in favor of legalization.

In a study by the American Bar Association, several proposals were put forth to deal with the underground economy. Following is a brief summary of some of the points:

1. Tax benefits available to a payer of cash would be conditional on his willingness to identify the payee.
2. Information reporting requirements should be instituted that would apply only to payments made in clash.
3. Informants and amnesty programs should be used.
4. Current criteria for reporting cash deposits and withdrawals should be made more stringent.
5. On income tax returns, the reporting of currency receipts separately from income received in the form of checks or credit cards should be required.
6. Any merchant or person providing goods or services and receiving payment in cash should be required to file an information return if the amount of currency received in any transaction exceeds a threshold amount.
7. Covert techniques should be used by the IRS, such as purchasing tax shelters, sting operations, use of computer data banks, and consensual monitoring. "Agents posing as potential buyers of restaurants and other small businesses . . . have been able to discover skimming of unreported cash receipts, inventory manipulation and other schemes that would not generally be picked up by audit procedures or information reporting."[34]

Some of the above proposals smack of Big Brotherism and should not be tolerated in a democratic society; others may well be implemented without too great an abridgment of every citizen's right to privacy. Whenever possible, the "stick" should be a strong and highly visible one.

NOTES

1. Robert Alford and Edgar Feige, "Information Distortions in Social Systems: The Underground Economy and Other Observer-Subject-Policymaker Feedbacks," in *The Underground Economies*, ed. Edgar Feige (Cambridge University Press), 67.

2. Peter Gutmann, "The Subterranean Economy, Redux," in *The Economics of the Shadow Economy*, ed. Wulf Gaertner and Alois Wenig (New York: Springer Verlag, 1985), 15.

3. Alford and Feige, *The Underground Economics*, 62.

4. Ibid., 71.

5. Edgar Feige, "The Meaning and Measurement of the Underground Economy," in *The Underground Economies.*

6. Robert Parker, "Informal Adjustments for Misreporting Tax Return Information Used to Estimate the National Income and Product Accounts, 1977," *Survey of Current Business* (June 1984), 17 and 18.

7. Robert McGee and Edgar Feige, "Policy Illusion, Macroeconomic Instability and the Unrecorded Economy," in *The Underground Economies*, loc. cit. p. 84.

8. David J. Pyle, "*Tax Evasion and the Black Economy*," (London: Macmillan, 1989) 144.

9. Robert D. Hershey, Jr., "Billions Elude Dollar Talley; Is Currency in Use Abroad?" *New York Times*, February 20, 1990, D3.

10. Peter Gutmann, *The Economics of the Shadow Economy*, 11.

11. For a balanced view of these issues, *see* Norman N. Bowsher, "The Demand for Currency: Is the Underground Economy Undermining Monetary Policy?" *Federal Revenue Bank of St. Louis, Review*, Vol. 62, No. 1 (January 1980), throughout.

12. Joel F. Houston, "Estimating the Size and Implications of the Underground Economy," Working Paper No. 87–91 Federal Reserve Bank of Philadelphia, Research Department, June 1987, pp 5–6.

13. Michael O'Higgins, "The Relationship Between the Formal and Hidden Economies: An Exploratory Analysis for Four Countries," in *The Economics of the Shadow Economy*, 130.

14. Ibid., 140.

15. James Alm, "The Welfare Cost of the Underground Economy," *Economic Inquiry* (April 1985): 244.

16. Robert M. Bleiberg, "Look Underground", *Barrons* (March 1, 1982), 11.

17. Robert D. Hershey, Jr., "Underground Economy Is Not Rising to the Bait," *New York Times*, January 24, 1988, sec. 4, col. 1.

18. Ibid.

19. *New York Times*, August 2, 1989, D22.

20. Stephen Lea, R. Tarpey, and Paul Webley, *The Individual in the Economy* (Cambridge University Press, 1987), 317.

21. David J. Pyle, Tax Evasion, 136.

22. O'Higgins, *The Economics of the Shadow Economy*, 140.

23. Telephone conversation with the Statistics of Income Division of the Internal Revenue Service.

24. Robert Mason and Lyle D. Calvin, "A Study of Admitted Income Tax Evasion," *Law and Society Review*, vol. 13, No. 1 (Fall 1978): 73.

25. Frank A. Cowell, *Cheating the Government* (Cambridge, Mass.: MIT Press, 1990), 108.

26. Ibid.

27. Peter Gutmann, "The Subterranean Economy: An Open Secret," *New Jersey Bill Journal*, vol. 4, No. 3 (Fall 1981): 39.

28. Donald R. Cressey, *Organized Crime and Criminal Organizations* (Cambridge, England: W. Heffer and Sons, 1971): 22.

29. Ibid., 22–23.

30. Thomas C. Schelling, "Economics and Criminal Enterprise," *The Public Interest* (Spring 1967: 76.

31. Mark H. Moore, *Buy and Bust* (Lexington, MA: Lexington Books, D. C. Heath and Co., 1977), 238.

32. Anthony Herman, Roger Lewis, and Tim Malyon, *Big Deal: The Politics of Illicit Drug Business* (London: Pluto Press, 1985), 100.

33. Roger Matthews, "Beyond Wolfenden? Prostitution, Politics and the Law," in *Confronting Crime*, ed. Roger Matthews and Jack Young. (Newbury Park, CA: Sage Publications, 1986), 193.

34. Gerald A. Feffer, Richard E. Trumble, Allen J. Weiner, and Martin L. Ernst, "Proposals to Deter and Detect the Underground Cash Economy," in American Bar Association, "Income Tax Compliance," a Report to the ABA Section of Taxation, May 16–19, 1983, p. 313.

8

Trail's End: Conclusion

We have arrived at the end of the major trails along which clues to the underground economy were pursued only to find that the goal is still an elusive one: that goal being a general consensus concerning the definition, size, and growth of underground economic activity. I have attempted to define the underground economy in a way that is consistent with the categories in our National Income and Product Accounts, namely[1] goods and services currently produced, the values of which are not caught in the statistical net and do not therefore become part of the Gross National (or Domestic) Product for a given period. The best approach, I thought, to deriving the dollar amounts omitted from the national accounts was (following Carl Simon and Ann Witte and Abt Associates) the sectorial one rather than those using variants of the money supply or transaction techniques. As a result both of the definition employed and the building block method of aggregation, the estimate presented in Chapter 4 is on the lower bound of most estimates of the U.S. underground economy. Nonetheless, the roughly $350 billion (6.7 percent of 1990s GNP) is not inconsiderable nor is the $50 billion shortfall in tax revenues insignificant.

Unlike Edgar Feige and Peter Gutmann, who began their investigations with the preconception that the underground economy was smaller than had been supposed and who discovered that it was larger (and more disconcerting), I began from the opposite premise, namely that the underground economy was far larger than had been commonly thought and came to the conclusion that it was smaller!

It is incumbent on those who use GNP and its associated measures in their work to develop more refined measurement techniques, so that the large gap between the lower and upper bounds of the various estimates may be narrowed. It is reassuring to note that the Bureau of Economic Analysis has set up a separate group to research these issues.

Since the evasion of taxes is a prime motive for going underground, a reform of the tax system in the direction of greater progressivity is in order so that the proverbial man (or woman) in the street is convinced that all of the actors in our economy are paying their fair share. In addition, since the benefit-cost ratio of the tax audits is favorable (anywhere from 3 to 5 to 1), the Internal Revenue Service should undertake much more of them and mete out more drastic penalties than now exist for the outright cheaters. Lest we go too far in this direction, however, it is well to heed Frank Cowell's admonition: "The public's revulsion at the prospect of a police state may be stronger than its appetite for the goods and services that the missing tax would have financed."[2]

I am acutely aware that the estimates presented in Table 4.4 are subject to debate, with some believing them too high, and others not high enough. Moreover, there undoubtedly exist more types of underground activity (even according to our narrow definition) than those enumerated. The gauntlet is down, however, and the more that researchers can bring to light, the better.

A disturbing problem exists in the area of monetary policy, since currency outflows associated primarily with the drug trade represent a partial loss of control over the money supply—a situation that the Treasury and the Federal Reserve authorities should attempt seriously to rectify.

I am convinced that an economy that is growing at a sound rate (in real per capita terms) and one in which job creation matches the growth of the labor supply, if not exceeds it somewhat, will diminish, but not entirely eliminate, incentives to underground activity. Drugs, gambling, prostitution, and pornography are activities that a healthy economy alone will not suffice to diminish or eliminate.

Arnold Heertji, Margaret Allen, and Harry Cohen wrote an interesting little book on the "black economy," and although its content was meant to apply primarily to the United Kingdom, the following excerpt applies with equal, if not greater force, to the United States:

> The unofficial economy can no longer be called an occasional and negligible phenomenon. Our society is pervaded by it. People are withdrawing into their own private worlds, society is becoming more and more anti-social, the citizen is becoming alienated from the community, the call for solidarity remains unheeded, people distrust the authorities and any form of power in general, identification with the community is decreasing and human contact is becoming grim and humorless. In such a climate deceiving the authorities is seen less and less as an offense and more and more as a sign of skill and enterprising spirit. People used to be ashamed of tax evasion, now they are proud of it."[3]

Unfortunately, the economists' armamentarium is inadequate to deal with the kinds of societal pathologies mentioned above. What is needed, as was stated previously, is a concerted interdisciplinary approach to the many ramifications of the underground economy. As economists, our task is to agree on definitions, to refine estimating techniques, and to indicate the benefits and costs of alternative approaches to the problem. Our contribution is not the only one but is a *sine qua non* of progress toward optimal solutions. I trust that this relatively brief volume will play some part in the ongoing discussion.

NOTES

1. Edgar L. Feige, "How Big Is the Irregular Economy?" *Challenge* (Nov./Dec. 1979): Peter Gutmann, "Statistical Illusions, Mistaken Policies," same source.

2. Frank A. Cowell, *Cheating the Government: The Economics of Evasion* (Cambridge, Mass.: The MIT Press, 1990), 154.

3. Arnold Heertji, Margaret Allen, and Harry Cohen, *The Black Economy* (London: Pam Books, 1982), 153–54.

Bibliography

Abt Associates. *Unreported Taxable Income from Selected Illegal Activities*, prepared for the Internal Revenue Service, U.S.G.P.O. September, 1984.

Alford, Robert R., and Edgar L. Feige. "Informal Distortions in Social Systems: The Underground Economy and Other Observer-Subject-Policymaker Feedbacks." In *Underground Economies*, edited by E. Feige (*See* under Feige).

Allan Guttmacher Institute. "Induced Abortions, A World Review, 1986," New York 1986, p. 43.

Alm, James. "The Welfare Cost of the Underground Economy," *Economic Inquiry* (April 1985): 244.

Benton, Lauren A. "Industrial Subcontracting and the Informal Sector: The Politics of Restructuring in the Madrid Electronics Industry." In *The Informal Economy*, edited by Alejandro Portes, Manuel Castells, and Lauren A. Benton. Baltimore and London: The Johns Hopkins University Press, 1989.

Bequar, August. *The Cashless Society: EFTS at the Crossroads*. New York: John Wiley and Sons, 1981.

Bierbaum, Tom. "Anti-Piracy Raids on the Rise but They Make Little Impact on $1 Billion Loss," *Variety*, April 4, 1990, 37.

Blades, Derek. "The Hidden Economy and National Accounts," The OECD Observer (January 1982): 15.

———. "The Hidden Economy and the National Accounts," *OECD Economic Outlook*, (June 1982): 28–45.

Bleiburg, Robert M., "Look Underground," *Barrons* (March 1, 1982): 11.

Boeschoten, W. C., and M. M. G. Fase. "The Volume of Payments and the Informal Economy of the Netherlands." *Monetary Monographs*, No. 1 De Nederlandsche Bank, Martinus Nijhoff Publishers, Dordrecht, 1984.

Bowsher, Norman N. "The Demand for Currency: Is the Underground Economy Undermining Monetary Policy?" *Federal Reserve Bank of St. Louis, Review* Vol. 62 No. 1 (January 1980).

Cagan, Philip, "The Demand for Currency Relative to Total Money Supply," *Occasional Paper 62, National Bureau of Economic Research*, New York, 1958.

Carson, Carol S., "The Underground Economy: An Introduction," *Survey of Current Business*, U.S. Department of Commerce, Bureau of Economic Analysis, Vol. 64, No. 5, May 1984 and July 1984.

———. "Gross National Product and Related Measures." In *The Handbook of Economic and Financial Measures*, edited by Frank J. Fabozzi and Harry I. Greenfield. Homewood, Ill.: Dow Jones-Irwin, 1984.

Carter, Michael. "The Hidden Economy: What Are the Issues?" *Discussion Paper No. 84 The Australian National University, Centre for Economic Policy Research*, December 1983.

Chambliss, William J. "The Political Economy of Smack: Opiates, Capitalism and Law," *Research in Laws and Sociology*, Vol. 1, 1978 p. 132.

Clark, Garcia, ed. *Traders Versus the State: Anthropological Approaches to the Unofficial Economies*. Boulder and London: Westview Press, 1988, Chapters 5 and 6.

Comptroller General. Report to the Congress, "Illegal Aliens, Estimating Their Impact on the United States," General Accounting Office, March 14, 1980 (processed).

Cowell, Frank A. *Cheating the Government*. Cambridge, Mass.: MIT Press, 1990.

Cressey, Donald R. *Organized Crime and Criminal Organizations*. Cambridge, England: W. Heffer and Sons, 1971.

De Grazia, Rafaele. *Clandestine Employment*, International Labor Office, Geneva, 1984, p. 14.

Denison, Edward F. "Is U.S. Growth Underestimated Because of the Underground Economy? Employment Ratios Suggest Not," *Review of Income and Wealth*, Series 28, No. 1, March 1982.

Soto, Hernando de. *The Other Path*. New York: Harper and Row, 1989. Economic Report of the President. Washington, D.C.: U.S.G.P.O. February 1990 and 1991.

Federal Reserve System. *Board of Governors*, "The Effects on Consumers and Creditors of Proposed Ceilings on Credit Card Interest Rates," *Staff Study 154*, October 1987, p 6.

Feffer, Gerald, A. et al. "Proposals to Deter and Detect the Underground Cash Economy," *Income Tax Compliance; A Report of the American Bar Association Section of Taxation*, May 18–19, 1983, p. 313.

Feige, Edgar L. ed. *The Underground Economies: Tax Evasion and Information Distortion*. New York: Cambridge University Press, 1989.

———. "How Big Is the Irregular Economy?" *Challenge*, November/December 1979.

———. "A Re-Examination of the Underground Economy in the United States," International Monetary Fund Staff Papers, 33, December 1986, p. 779.

———. "The Meaning and Measurement of the Underground Economy." In *The Underground Economies*.

Ferman, Louis A., Louise E. Berndt, and Elaine Selo. "Analysis of the Irregular Economy: Cash Flows in the Informal Sector," *Institute of Labor and Industrial Relations, University of Michigan-Wayne State University*, March 1978 (mimeographed).

———. "The Irregular Economy." In *Can I Have It in Cash*, edited by Stuart Henry. London: Astragal Books, 1981.

Ferman, Louis, Stuart Henry, and Michele Hoyman. "Issues and Prospects for the Study of Informal Economies: Concepts, Research, Strategies and Policy," *The Informal Economy, Annals of the American Academy of Political and Social Science* (September 1987), 168.

Foreman, Julia. "Can We End the Shame? Recent Multilateral Efforts to Address the World Child Pornography Market," *Vanderbilt Journal of Transnational Law*, Vol. 23, No. 2 (1990): 439.

Freud, Sigmond. "Civilization and Its Discontents." In *A Freud Reader*, edited by Peter Gay, New York: W. W. Norton, 1989.

Frey, Bruno S. See Hanneman.

Gaertner, Wulf and Alois Wenig, eds. *The Economics of the Shadow Economy*," Proceedings, Bielefeld, West Germany, Springer Verlag, Berlin 1985.

Garcia, Gillian. "The Currency Ratio and the Subterranean Economy," *Financial Analysis Journal* (November/December 1978): 66.

Goldfield, Stephen. "The Case of the Missing Money," *Brookings Papers on Economic Activity*, No. 3, Brookings Institution, Washington, D.C. 1976, p. 720.

Gutmann, Peter. "The Subterranean Economy," *Financial Analysts Journal* (November/December 1977).

———. "Statistical Illusions, Mistaken Policies," *Challenge* (November/December 1979).

———. "Are the Unemployed Unemployed?" *Financial Analysts Journal* (September/October 1978).

———. "The Grand Unemployment Illusion," *The Journal of the Institute for Socioeconomic Studies*,. No. 2 (Summer 1979).

———. "The Subterranean Economy: An Open Secret," *New Jersey Bell Journal*, Vol. 4, No. 3, (Fall 1981): 39.

———. "The Subterranean Economy, Redux," in *The Economics of the Shadow Economy* (*See* W. Gaertner).

Hanneman-Weck, Hannalore and Bruno S. Frey. "Measuring the Shadow Economy: The Case of Switzerland." in *The Economics of the Shadow Economy*. Table 11, p. 100.

Harding, Philip and Richard Jenkins. *The Myth of the Hidden Economy* (Philadelphia: University Press, 1989).

Heertji, Arnold, Margaret Allen, and Harry Cohen. *The Black Economy*. London: Pam Brooks, 1982.

Hendrickson, Robert A. *The Cashless Society*. New York: Dodd Mead and Co., 1972.

Henry, James. "Calling in the Big Bills," *Washington Monthly* (May 1976): 31.

Herman, Anthony, Roger Lewis, and Ti Malyon. *Big Deal: The Politics of the Illicit Drug Business*. London: Pluto Press, 1985.

Hershey, Robert D., Jr. "Billions Elude Dollar Tally: Is the Currency in Use Abroad?" *New York Times*, February 20, 1990, D3.

———. "Underground Economy is Not Rising to the Bait," *New York Times*, January 24, 1988 sec. 4 col. 1.

Hillberger, C. and H. Kuepal. "How Big Is the Shadow Economy?" *European Economic Review*, Vol. 32 (1988): p. 971.

Houston, Joel. F. "Estimating the Size and Implications of the Underground Economy," *Working Paper 87–9 Federal Reserve Bank of Philadelphia*, Research Department, June 1987.

Internal Revenue Service, "Estimates of Income Unreported on Individual Income Tax Returns," Department of Treasury, *Publication 1104*, September 1979.

———. "Income Tax Compliance Research," *Department of the Treasury, Publication 7285*, March 1988.

Jaffe, Frederick S., B. Lindheim, and Philip R. Lee. *Abortion Politics*. New York: McGraw Hill Books, 1981.

Keynes, J. M. *The General Theory of Employment, Interest and Money*. London: Mcmillan, 1936.

Kuznets, Simon. "National Income: A Summary of Findings," *National Bureau of Economic Research*, 1946.

Lea, Stephen, R. Tarpey, and P. Webley. *The Individual in the Economy*. Cambridge University Press, 1987.

Levitan, S. A. and Clifford M. Johnson. *Second Thoughts on Work*, W. E. Upjohn Institute for Employment Research, Kalamazoo, Mich., 1982, p. 53.

Lubell, Harold. *The Informal Sector in 1980's and 1990's*. Paris: OECD, 1991.

Lyman, Michael D. *Gangland: Drug Trafficking by Organized Criminals*. Springfield, Ill.: C. C. Thomas, 1989.

Maital, Shlomo. "Only the Shadow Knows the Underground Economy's Real Size," *Barrons* (November 14, 1983): 16.

Mason, Robert and Lyle Calvin. "A Study of Admitted Income Tax Evasion," *Law and Society Review*, Vol. 12 No. 1 (1978): 73.

Mattera, Philip. *Off the Books: The Rise of the Underground Economy*. New York: St. Martin's Press, 1985.

Matthews, Roger. "Beyond Wolfenden? Prostitution, Politics and the Law." In *Confronting Crime*, ed. Roger Matthews and Jack Young. Newbury Park, CA: Sage Publications, 1986.

McRohan, Kevin F. and James D. Smith. "Informal Suppliers in the Underground Economy," *Statistics of Income Bulletin*, (SOI) (Summer, 1983).

McDonald, Richard J. "The Underground Economy and BLS Statistical Data," *Monthly Labor Review* (January 1984): 16.

McGee, Robert and E. Feige. "Policy Illusion, Macroeconomic Instability and the Unrecorded Economy." In *The Underground Economies*, edited by E. Feige.

Mills, James. *The Underground Empire: Where Crime and Government Embrace*. Garden City: Doubleday, 1986.

Mirus, Rolf and Roger S. Smith. "Canada's Underground Economy." In *The Underground Economies*, edited by E. Feige.

Molefsky, Barry. America's Underground Economy, *Report No. 81–181E Congressional Research Service*, The Library of Congress, Washington, D.C.

Moore, Mark H. *Buy and Bust*. Lexington, MA: Lexington Books, D. C. Heath and Co., 1977.

New York Times, March 3, 1991, p. 1. April 20, 1990, p. D1. April 26, 1990. November 7, 1990, p. A27. November 26, 1990, p. D4. April 13, 1991, p. 50. April 17, 1991, p. D1. August 2, 1989, p. D22. Dec. 5, 1991, p. D13.

O'Brien, Shirley. *Child Pornography*. Dubuque, Iowa: Kendal Hunt Publishing Co., 1983.

Office of National Drug Control Policy. *What America's Users Spend on Illegal Drugs*, Technical Paper, June 1991.

O'Higgins, Michael. "The Relationship Between the Formal and the Hidden Economies," "An Exploratory Analysis for Four Countries" in *Economics of the Shadow Economy*, p. 130.

O'Neil, David. "Growth of the Underground Economy, 1950–81, Some Evidence from the Current Population Survey," *Joint Economics Committee*, December 9, 1983, p. 13.

Parker, Robert. "Informal Adjustments for Misreporting Tax Return Information Used to Estimate the National Income and Product Accounts, 1977," *Survey of Current Business* (June 1984): 17 and 18.

Porter, Richard D. and Amanda S. Bayer. "A Monetary Perspective on Underground Economic Activity in the United States," *Federal Reserve Bulletin* (March 1984): 187.

President's Commission on Organized Crime, Report to the President and the Attorney General. *America's Habit: Drug Abuse, Drug Trafficking and Organized Crime*," U.S.G.P.O. March 1986 p. 5 and note 2.

———. *Organized Crime and Gambling*, U.S.G.P.O. June 1985.

Pyle, David J. *Tax Evasion and the Black Economy*. London: Macmillan, 1989.

Revell, J. R. S. *Banking and Electronic Fund Transfers*. Paris: OECD, 1983.

Reynolds, Helen. *The Economics of Prostitution*. Springfield, Ill.: Charles C. Thomas, 1986.

Schelling, Thomas C. "Economics and Criminal Enterprise," *Public Interest* (Spring 1967): 76.

Select Committee on Narcotics Abuse and Control. *Annual Report*, January 3, 1991.

Sethuramen, S. V., ed. *The Urban Informal Sector in Developing Countries*. Geneva: International Labor Office, 1981.

Simon, Carl P. and Ann D. Witte. *Beating the System*. "The Underground Economy." Boston, Mass.: Auburn House Publishing Company, 1982.

Smith, Stephen. *Britain's Shadow Economy*. Oxford: Clarendon Press, 1986.

Soiffer, Stephen S. and Gretchen M. Hermann. *Sociological Review*, 35 (February 1987): 49–50.

Stein, Bruno. "Subterranean Labor Markets: A Conceptual Analysis," in *The Economics of the Shadow Economy*, *See* Gaertner and Wenig.

Tanzi, Vito. "The Underground Economy and Tax Evasion in the United States, Estimates and Implications." In *The Underground Economy in the United States and Abroad*, edited by Vito Tanzi, Lexington, Mass.: Lexington Books, D. C. Heath and Co., 1982.

Tighe, Carla. "The Underground Economy," *Illinois Business Review* (April 1985): 10.

Treasury Bulletin (March 1991): 137.

U.S. House of Representatives, Committee on Ways and Means, Subcommittee on Oversight, "Underground Economy," July 16, 1979.

U.S. News and World Report. "How Tax Cheaters Get Away with Billions," March 27, 1978.

Wall Street Journal, April 3, 1978. April 10, 1978. April 24, 1978. April 3, 1991. May 17, 1991. July 5, 1979.

Index

Abortion, 61, 112
Abt Associates, 51, 57, 60, 123
Alford, Robert R., 105, 106
Allen, Margaret, 125
American Bar Association, 114, 120
Annals of the American Academy of Political and Social Science, 74
Argentina, 101
Australia, 94
Austria, 94

Bank of Credit & Commerce Intl., 55
Bartering, 10, 63
Benton, Lauren A., 98
Blades, Derek, 13, 35
Bleiberg, Robert M., 114

Cagan, Philip, 25
Canada, 110
Carson, Carol S., 35, 45
Carter, Michael, 23, 98
Castells, Manuel, 98
Cigarette smuggling, 11, 63, 112
Cohen, Harry, 125
Confederation of Independent States, 14
Cowell, Frank A., 13, 117, 124
Cressey, Donald E., 118
Cycles, 109, 110

De Grazia, Rafaele, 74, 88
Denison, Edward F., 83, 84
De Soto, Hernando, 101
Do-it-yourself, 10
Drugs, 7, 111

Economic Efficiency, 113
Employment-to-Population Ratio, 83
European Economic Community (EEC), 97

European Parliament, 55

Federal Reserve System, 20, 24, 124
Feige, Edgar L., 27, 96, 105, 106, 107, 108, 124
France, 94
Frey, Bruno S., 96, 97

Gambling, 7, 9, 111
Garcia, Gillian, 26
Germany, 110
Ghana, 100
Goldfeld, Stephen, 26
Gross Domestic Product (GDP), 93
Gross National Product (GNP), 2
Gutmann, Peter, 25, 35, 37, 78, 80, 85, 108, 118, 124
Guyana, 100

Hanneman-Weck, Hannalore, 96, 97, 139
Heertji, Arnold, 125
Hendrickson, Robert A., 21
Henry, James, 24
Heroin, 54
Hershey, Robert D., Jr., 108
Hillberger, C., 82
House Select Committee on Narcotics Use and Control, 53
Houston, Joel F., 29

Illegal aliens, 87
India, 100
Informal economy, 98
Internal Revenue Service (IRS), 40, 51, 124; Taxpayer Compliance Measurement Program (TCMP) of, 39
Israel, 100
Italy, 96, 103 n.7

Japan, 94

Kuepal, H., 82
Kuznets, Simon, 3, 16 n.4

Labor force participation rate, 78
Levitan, S. A., 81
Loan sharking, 9, 63, 112
Long, Susan, 98
Lubell, Harold, 98

Macroeconomic approach, 35
Mafia, 15
Maital, Shlomo, 22
Marijuana, 54
Mattera, Phillip, 14, 15, 39, 74
McDonald, Richard J., 77, 85, 86
McGee, Robert, 108
Microeconomic approach, 35
Molefsky, Barry, 74, 82, 88
Money laundering, 55
Money supply, 23; velocity of, 26
Moore, Mark H., 119
Mustang Ranch, 59

National Income and Product Accounts (NIPA), 2, 45
Netherlands, 119

Organization for Economic Cooperation and Development (OECD), 20, 97, 98
Off-the-books, 7, 9, 74, 112
O'Higgins, Michael, 110, 116

Parker, Robert, 108
Peru, 100
Piracy, 62, 112
Pornography, 62, 111
Portes, Alejandro, 98
President's Commission on Organized Crime, 53, 57
Prostitution, 7, 58, 111
Pyle, David J., 29, 84, 115

Rand, Rebecca, 58
Resource shifts: Autonomous and induced, 113
Revell, J.R.S., 20
Reynolds, Helen, 58

Savings and Loan, 4
Schelling, Thomas C., 119
Select Committee on Narcotics Abuse, Annual Report, 53
Self-employed, 80
Simon, Carl P., 51, 63, 123
Skimming, 11, 63
Smith, Adam, 56
Smith, Stephen, 30
Soviet Union, 18. *See also* Confederation of Independent States
Spain, 96
Stein, Bruno, 3
Sweden, 96
Switzerland, 94

Taiwan, 100
Tanzania, 100
Tanzi, Vito, 28, 29
Taxes: Evasion, 38, 40, 114; Marginal rates, 115; Morality, 117
Tighe, Carla, 4
Transactions approach, 27

Underground economy of New York State, 65
Underground economy of the U.S.: definition of, 2; typology of, 8; size, estimate of, 64; economic consequences of, 105–120
Underground labor force, 73
United Kingdom, 110
United States (relative ranking), 94
United States Department of Commerce: Bureau of the Census, 76; Bureau of Economic Analysis, 95; Current Population Survey, 76
United States Department of Labor: Bureau of Labor Statistics, 76; United States General Accounting Office, 87; Committee on Ways and Means, Subcommittee on Oversight, 38
United States Treasury Department, 55
U.S. News and World Report, 36

Witte, Ann D., 51, 63, 123

About the Author

HARRY I. GREENFIELD is Professor Emeritus of Economics at Queens College of the City University of New York. He is the author of several books including *Manpower and the Growth of Producer Services* (1966).